THE ENGLISH COUNTRY CRAFTS COLLECTION

THE ENGLISH COUNTRY CRAFTS COLLECTION

JULIA JONES AND BARBARA DEER

Photographs by Jon Davison

By the same authors
ROYAL PLEASURES AND PASTIMES
Crafts from the Royal Courts

A DAVID & CHARLES CRAFT BOOK

From Barbara
'for my god-daughter Cherry'
and
from Julia
'for Mark, Mandy and Adam'

British Library Cataloguing in Publication Data
Jones, Julia *1945–*
  The English country crafts collection.
  1. England. Rural crafts
  I. Title   II. Deer, Barbara
  680.942

ISBN 0–7153–9847–4

Typeset by Ace Filmsetting Ltd, Frome, Somerset
and printed in The Netherlands by RotoSmeets Offset
for David & Charles plc
Brunel House   Newton Abbot   Devon

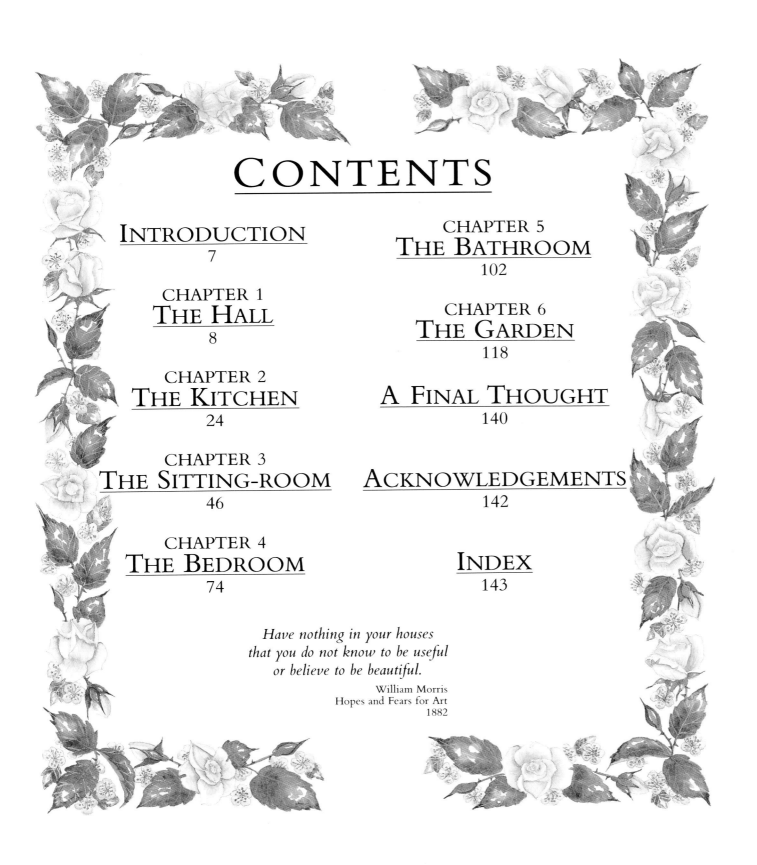

CONTENTS

*Have nothing in your houses
that you do not know to be useful
or believe to be beautiful.*

William Morris
Hopes and Fears for Art
1882

In this rare Art, yet here they may discerne
Some things to teach them if they list to learne.
And as this booke some cunning workes doth teach,
(Too hard for meane capacities to reach)
So for weake learners, other workes here be,
As plaine and easie as are ABC.
Thus skillfull, or unskillfull, each make take
This booke, and of it each goode use may make,
All sortes of workes, almost that can be nam'd,
Here are directions how they may be fram'd . . .

John Taylor
'The Prayse of the Needle'

INTRODUCTION

ODAY'S IDEAL COUNTRY COTTAGE is a happy jumble of things old and new – a home where the latest technology can sit comfortably side by side with the treasures and bric-à-brac of the past.

However, the idyllic dream home of the city-dweller, with its roses around the porch and its doves cooing on the roof is, for many, an impossible fantasy. Nevertheless, the homely atmosphere of this cottage paradise can, with a little ingenuity and imagination, be easily reproduced in most settings. Using the many and varied skills of the past, it is possible to create the warm and welcoming environment that is so necessary to come home to in today's demanding high-technology society. In creating this comfortable ambience, the secret of success lies, not in the bricks and mortar of your home, but in those thoughtful, additional touches, which will reflect your personality and testify to the love and time you have been prepared to invest in your surroundings.

How many of us have driven through a quiet English village at dusk, enviously trying to peep through little casement windows to catch a glimpse of the inviting rooms inside? The warm glow of table lamps and the flicker of firelight seem to capture all that is English – bringing back, perhaps, happy memories of almost forgotten winter tea-times round the fire. This collection of crafts seeks to capture the spirit of the English country cottage, in the hope that each project you undertake will contain a little of your personality and will, therefore, make each creation something of which to be justly proud.

Do not feel that the instructions must be rigidly adhered to – rather use them as a guide and inspiration. Each item will then become a family heirloom to cherish, enriching and embellishing your home.

CHAPTER 1
THE HALL

When you open the front door you have to feel welcome.
If you get that feeling at the very beginning,
you tend to dismiss other aspects of the house
that may not be so nice.

Ronald Grimaldi, Designer

THE HALL – often the first room that the visitor sees – is probably the most difficult to decorate and furnish. A country cottage hall should be warm and welcoming to guests and family alike and should reflect and echo the spirit of the whole house.

If space permits, a small table can act as a focal point, displaying an array of little treasures and trinkets. In a Victorian home, this would have included a small tray on to which a visitor might drop her calling card. Today, this tray might carry a potted fern, adding a touch of freshness and coolness with its delicate green foliage.

A selection of handmade accessories will add a touch of warmth and personality to what could be a very bland room. Decorative interest can be added to the walls by hanging them with a selection of pictures and *objets d'art*, while the homely atmosphere can be increased by the use of bunches of dried flowers, twig circles and fir cones in small baskets.

FIRST IMPRESSIONS
This collection of hall table trinkets includes a decorative Dorset
button and family photographs displayed in unusual fabric-covered
frames. An imaginative stencilled mirror completes the picture

STENCILLED MIRROR

MATERIALS

tracing paper
1 2B lead pencil
15 × 15cm/6 × 6in piece of stencil card (impregnated with linseed oil)
cutting board
craft knife
1 framed mirror, any size or shape, (the frame can be of wood, metal or plastic)
ruler
adhesive tape or Blutack
stencil brush
1 small tin enamel paint in each:
peach
olive green

METHOD

1 To make a stencil, trace the design shown in the diagram on to tracing paper, using the 2B pencil.
2 Lay the tracing paper over the stencil card and carefully draw over the outline of the design, transferring the pattern to the card.
3 Using the cutting board, or several newspapers on a wooden board, carefully cut round the design using the craft knife fitted with a new blade. The stencil is now ready to be used.
4 If a rectangular frame is being used, carefully mark the centre point of each side with a light pencil mark.
5 Secure the stencil to the frame, starting close to the centre point, using either the adhesive tape or small pieces of Blutack. Make sure that the stencil lies flat against the frame and is firmly in place before starting to paint.
6 Using the peach enamel paint in the appropriate areas, start to transfer the stencil design with the stencil brush. Then apply the green paint to the remaining areas. Leave each section to dry before removing the stencil and working the next pattern repeat. In this way work out to one corner.
7 Turn stencil over, making sure that the paint is completely dry, and again work from the centre point out to the opposite corner.
8 Repeat the above instructions on the remaining three sides.

If you are using a round or oval frame, it is as well to plan out the entire design in pencil, before starting to paint, so that you can be sure of the finished effect.

CROCHET TABLECLOTH

To ADD DECORATIVE EFFECT to any room, nothing looks more attractive than a hand-crocheted tablecloth. To be strictly traditional this should be made in white or ecru and will, therefore, tone with any decor. The yarn used to produce this cloth is not too fine and will work up quite quickly.

MATERIALS

9 × 50g balls of Twilleys Stalite in white or ecru
3.50 crochet hook

TENSION

1st 4 rounds to 9cm/3½in

ABBREVIATIONS

ch – chain
dc – double crochet [single crochet]*
tr – treble [double crochet]
sp – space
sl st – slip stitch
lp – loop
cont – continue
st – stitch
sts – stitches
in – inch/es
cm – centimetre/s
rep – repeat
grps – groups
*[USA equivalents]

MEASUREMENTS

Finished measurement of cloth is 114cm/45in diameter

METHOD

Important: work into the back loop of every stitch and every chain throughout.

With 3.50 crochet hook make 6 ch, sl st to 1st ch to form a ring.

1st round: 3 ch (standing as 1st tr) 12 tr into ring, sl st to top of 3 ch.

2nd round: 3 ch, 2 tr into each tr to end, sl st to top of 3 ch (25 sts).

3rd round: 3 ch, 2 tr into each tr to end, sl st to top of 3 ch (51 sts).

4th round: 3 ch, 1 tr into each of next 2 tr (2 tr into next tr, 1 tr into each of next 2 tr) 16 times, sl st to top of 3 ch (67 sts).

5th round: 3 ch (2 tr into next tr, 3 tr) 16 times, 2 tr, sl st to top of 3 ch (83 sts).

6th round: 3 ch, 2 tr (2 tr in next tr, 4 tr) 16 times, sl st to top of 3 ch (99 sts).

7th round: 3 ch, 8 tr (2 tr into next tr, 6 tr) 13 times, sl st to top of 3 ch (112 sts).

8th round: 4 ch, miss 1 tr, (1 tr into next tr, 1 ch, miss 1 tr) to end, sl st to 3rd of 4th ch.

9th round: 4 ch (1 tr into next tr, 1 ch) to end, sl st to 3rd of 4 ch.

10th round: 3 ch, 2 tr into 1 ch (1 tr into tr, 2 tr into 1 ch) to end, sl st to top of 3 ch (168 sts).

11th round: 7 ch, miss 2 tr * 1 tr into next tr, miss 1 tr, 1 tr into each of next 15 tr, miss 1 tr, 1 tr in next tr, 4 ch, miss 2 tr, rep from * 7 times more, ending last rep with 15 tr, miss 1 tr, sl st to 3rd of 7 ch (8 grps).

12th round: Sl st into 4 ch sp, * 1 dc in 4 ch sp, 4 ch miss 1 tr, work 15 tr, 4 ch miss 1 tr, rep from * 7 times more, ending with sl st to 1st dc.

13th round: Sl st into next 4 ch sp, 1 dc into same sp, * 4 ch, miss 1 tr, work 13 tr (4 ch, 1 dc into next 4 ch sp) twice, rep from * 7 times more, ending sl st to 1st dc.

14th round: Sl st into next 4 ch sp, 1 dc into same sp, * 4 ch, miss 1 tr, work 11 tr, (4 ch, 1 dc into next 4 ch sp) 3 times, rep from * 7 times more, ending sl st into 1st dc.

15th round: Sl st into next 4 ch sp, 1 dc into same sp, * 4 ch, miss 1 tr, work 9 tr (4 ch, 1 dc into next 4 ch sp) 4 times, rep from * 7 times more, ending sl st into first dc.

16th round: Sl st into next 4 ch sp, 1 dc into same sp, * 4 ch, miss 1 tr, work 7 tr, (4 ch, 1 dc into next 4 ch sp) 5 times, rep from * 7 times more, ending sl st into first dc.

17th round: Sl st into next 4 ch sp, 1 dc into same sp, * 4 ch, miss 1 tr, work 5 tr, (4 ch, 1 dc into next 4 ch sp) 6 times, rep from * 7 times more, ending sl st into first dc.

18th round: Sl st into next 4 ch sp, 1 dc into same sp, * 4 ch, miss 1 tr, work 3 tr, (4 ch, 1 dc into next 4 ch sp) 7 times, rep from * 7 times more, ending sl st to first dc.

19th round: Sl st into next 4 ch sp, 1 dc into same sp, * 4 ch, miss 1 tr, 1 tr, (4 ch, 1 dc into next 4 ch sp) 8 times, rep from * 7 times more, ending sl st to first dc.

20th round: Sl st to centre of next 4 ch sp, 6 ch (1 tr into next 4 ch sp, 3 ch) to end, sl st to 3rd of 6 ch.

21st round: 6 ch, (1 tr into next tr, 3 ch) to end, sl st to 3rd of 6 ch.

22nd round: Sl st over next 3 ch and 1 tr into next 3 ch sp, 3 ch, 3 tr into same sp, 4 tr into each of next seven 3 ch sp, 3 ch, miss one 3 ch sp * 4 tr into each of next eight 3 ch sp, 3 ch, miss one 3 ch sp, rep from * 6 times more, sl st to top of 3 ch.

23rd round: 6 ch, * miss 2 tr, 1 tr into each of next 26 tr, 3 ch, miss 2 tr, 1 tr into next tr, 3 ch, 1 tr into next tr, 3 ch, rep from * 7 times more, ending 3 ch, sl st into 3rd of 6 ch.

24th round: 6 ch, 1 tr into next tr, 3 ch, * miss 2 tr, work 20 tr, 3 ch, miss 2 tr, (1 tr into next tr, 3 ch) 4 times, rep from * 7 times more, ending sl st into 3rd of 6 ch.

25th round: 6 ch, (1 tr into next tr, 3 ch) twice, * miss 2 tr, work 14 tr, 3 ch, miss 2 tr, (1 tr into next tr, 3 ch) 6 times, rep from * 7 times more, ending sl st to 3rd ch.

26th round: 6 ch, (1 tr into next tr, 3 ch) 3 times, *

miss 2 tr, work 8 tr, 3 ch, miss 2 tr, (1 tr into next tr, 3 ch) 8 times, rep from * 7 times more, ending sl st to 3rd of 6 ch.

27th round: 6 ch, (1 tr into next tr, 3 ch) 4 times, * miss 2 tr, work 2 tr, 3 ch, miss 2 tr, (1 tr into next tr, 3 ch) 10 times, rep from * 7 times more, ending sl st into 3rd of 6 ch.

28th round: Sl st into next 3 ch sp, 1 dc in same sp, (4 ch, 1 dc into next ch sp) 4 times, * 4 ch, 1 dc between 2 tr (4 ch, 1 dc into next 3 ch sp) 11 times, rep from * 7 times more, ending sl st into first dc (96 ch sps).

29th round: Sl st to centre of next ch sp, (5 ch, 1 dc into next ch sp) to end.

30th round: As 29th round.

31st round: Sl st to centre of next ch sp, (6 ch, 1 dc into next ch sp) to end.

32nd round: Sl st to centre of next ch sp, * 6 ch, 1 dc in same sp, (6 ch, 1 dc into next ch sp) 8 times, rep from * 11 times more (108 ch sps).

33rd round: * 4 ch, miss one 6 ch sp, work (3 tr, 1 ch, 3 tr) all into next 6 ch sp, 4 ch, miss one 6 ch sp, 1 dc into next dc rep from * to end (36 grps).

34th round: * 5 ch, work (3 tr, 1 ch, 3 tr) all into next 1 ch sp, 5 ch, 1 dc into next dc, rep from * to end.

35th round: As 34th round, working 6 ch instead of 5 ch.

36th round: As 34th round, working 7 ch instead of 5 ch.

37th round: Sl st over next 7 ch and 3 tr into 1 ch sp, 3 ch, (2 tr, 1 ch, 3 tr) all in the same sp, 8 ch, * work (3 tr, 1 ch, 3 tr) all in 1 ch sp, 8 ch, rep from * to end, sl st to top of 3 ch.

38th round: Sl st over next 2 tr and into 1 ch sp, 3 ch, 2 tr in same sp, * 1 ch, 11 tr into 8 ch sp, 1 ch, 3 tr into 1 ch sp, rep from * ending sl st to top of 3 ch.

39th round: Sl st over next 2 tr and into 1 ch sp, * 5 ch, miss 5 tr, 1 dc into next tr, 5 ch, miss 5 tr, 1 dc into 1 ch sp, 5 ch, miss 3 tr, 1 dc into 1 ch sp, rep from * to end (108 ch sps).

40th round: Sl st to centre of next ch sp, * 5 ch, 1 dc into same sp, (5 ch, 1 dc into next ch sp) 9 times, rep from * 11 times more (120 ch sps).

41st round: Sl st to centre of next ch sp (6 ch, 1 dc into next ch sp) to end.

42nd round: Sl st to centre of next ch sp, * 6 ch, 1 dc into same sp, (6 ch, 1 dc into next ch sp) 10 times, rep from * 11 times more (132 ch sps).

43rd round: As 41st round.

44th round: As 33rd round (44 grps).

45th to 49th rounds: As 34th to 38th rounds inclusive.

50th round: Sl st over next 2 tr and into 1 ch sp, * (5 ch, miss 3 tr, 1 dc into next tr) twice, (5 ch, miss 3 tr, 1 dc into next ch sp) twice, rep from * to end (176 ch sps).

51st round: Sl st to centre of next ch sp, (5 ch, 1 dc into next ch sp) to end.

52nd round: As 51st round.

53rd round: Sl st to centre of next ch sp, (6 ch, 1 dc into next ch sp) to end.

54th round: Sl st to centre of next ch sp, * 6 ch, 1 dc into same sp, (6 ch, 1 dc into next ch sp) 8 times, rep from * 21 times more (198 ch sps).

55th round: As 33rd round (66 grps).

56th to 58th rounds: As 34th to 36th rounds inclusive.
Fasten off.

FILET CROCHET CURTAIN

THE FRONT DOOR sets the style for the rest of the house, so what could be more suitable than this filet crochet curtain used against its bull's eye window?

Filet crochet was a popular pastime in Victorian and Edwardian times. The original designs were often based on sixteenth-century netted lacework. This curtain was originally designed for quite a small window, but the design could be adapted to produce a curtain to fit any size of window by simply increasing the number of scallop repeats to increase the width, or by altering the number of circle repeats to produce the desired length.

MATERIALS

7 × 20g balls of Twilleys crochet cotton No 40
1.00 crochet hook
9 small brass curtain rings
piece of dowelling (approx 74cm/29in)

MEASUREMENTS

Finished size is 82 × 56cm/32 × 22in approx

ABBREVIATIONS

ch – chain
dc – double crochet [single crochet]*
tr – treble [double crochet]
dbl tr – double treble [treble]
st – stitch
*[USA equivalents]

METHOD

(A block is formed by 1 dbl tr into following 3 ch. An open mesh is formed by 2 ch and one dbl tr into 3rd st from hook.)

Make a chain of 478 sts. Now make a foundation row as follows:

Work a tr into the 3rd chain from the hook. Then work a tr into each of the following 475 chain stitches (making 476 trs in all). Turn. Continue as follows:

Row 1: 4 ch (to form the first dbl tr) 1 dbl tr into each tr to end of row. Turn.

Rows 2 and 3: Rep row 1.

Row 4: 4 ch (to form the first dbl tr), * 2 ch, miss 2 dbl tr, 1 dbl tr, into next dbl tr repeat from * to end of row. Turn.

Now continue making meshes and blocks following the chart until row 111 is completed.

The curtain can be lengthened or shortened at this point by working more or less pattern repeats, always ending on row 16 of the chart.

To work the scalloped edge, decrease by slip stitching along top of last block of previous row, 4 ch, 3 dbl tr into following 3 sts. On alternate rows, simply omit last block of previous row.

Fasten off and sew in ends.

Wash and starch very lightly. Pin out to a rectangle 82 × 56cm/32 × 22in and leave to dry.

Attach 9 small brass rings at 8cm/3in intervals along the top edge of curtain by oversewing with crochet cotton.

Hang the curtain on wooden dowelling or brass rod.

THE HALL WINDOW
A delicate filet crochet curtain filters summer sunlight into the country cottage hallway

PHOTOGRAPH FRAMES

AS CAN BE SEEN from the photograph on page 9, the size of these frames can be varied to suit the photographs to be framed and can be decorated using any number of different edgings and ribbons.

By careful choice of fabrics an impressive and individual display can be produced for very little outlay in time or money. A half metre of fabric will make several frames, depending on their size.

MATERIALS

sheet of mount board 82 × 102cm/32 × 40in
ruler
soft lead pencil
set square
metal ruler
scalpel
0.5m/½yd medium-weight wadding 90cm/36in wide
craft glue
0.5m/½yd 90cm/36in printed cotton fabric
0.3m/⅜yd printed cotton fabric
(for the above fabrics choose toning or contrasting colours)
glass-headed pins
double-faced carpet tape
0.8m/⅞yd 3mm/⅛in satin cording
toning sewing thread
clothes pegs
small length of matching ribbon (optional)

MEASUREMENTS

Finished measurement is 15 × 22cm/6 × 8½in

METHOD

1 On mount board, using pencil and ruler, draw two rectangles measuring 15 × 22cm/6 × 8½in checking with the set square that the corners are accurate. Using the scalpel and a metal ruler, cut out these rectangles. Take one rectangle and measure in 4cm/1½in several times along each short side and 2.5cm/1in along each long side. Draw an inner rectangle, using these marks as your guideline. Again using the metal ruler and scalpel, cut out and discard this smaller rectangle to form a window approx 10 × 14cm/4 × 5½in.

2 Following instructions in step 1, cut a stand guide from the remaining mount board by cutting a rectangle measuring 15 × 5cm/6 × 2in. Measure in 0.75cm/¼in from each corner on one short end of rectangle, draw a line from opposite corner on same side to this point on both sides and cut. This will give you a slightly tapered piece of card.

3 Now cut four rectangles of wadding, using one rectangular piece of cut mount board (15 × 22cm/6 × 8½in) as your template.

4 Using craft glue, glue two layers of wadding to one side each of front and back mount-board rectangles. Leave to dry thoroughly before moving to the next step.

5 Using the scalpel cut out the small rectangle of wadding covering the window on the front mount board.

6 Again using a mount-board rectangle as your template, draw round on to wrong side of main piece of printed cotton fabric. As you do this, make sure that the template sits squarely on the fabric along the warp and weft lines. Now, using a ruler draw cutting lines on the fabric 1.5cm/½in outside these lines. These lines should also be drawn inside the rectangular window, and an additional line drawn from corner of mount to corner of seam line in each corner of fabric. This will allow for cutting turn backs in fabric when it is placed in position. Cut out carefully.

7 Lay mount-board front, padded side down, over the wrong side of the fabric. Pull seam allowance through opening to wrong side. Glue in place, holding the edge in place with pins. Leave to dry.

8 Apply double-faced tape to wrong side of front, close to all outer edges.

9 With wrong side towards you, pull front fabric smoothly over wadding and press edges against the

tape. Clip curves and trim corners as needed. Check that the fabric is smooth on the right side.

10 Glue satin cording to front along outer edge, tapering one end behind the other, as shown in diagram 1.

Diagram 1

11 Lay the contrasting fabric, right side down, on to a flat surface and, using the second rectangle as a template, draw round this and cut out. Glue wrong side of lining fabric to unpadded side of mount-board back. Leave to dry.

12 Lay the remaining main colour fabric right side down on a flat surface and, again using this rectangle as a template, draw another rectangle, allowing a seam turning of 1.25cm/½in all round. Cut out.

13 Apply double-faced tape to the unpadded side of the back rectangle over lining fabric and close to all edges.

14 Lay mount-board back, padded side down, over wrong side of remaining fabric rectangle.

15 With right side towards you, pull fabric smoothly over wadding and press edges against tape. Clip curves and trim corners as needed. Be sure the fabric is smooth on the right side.

16 Make mount-board spacers by glueing 1.25cm/½in wide mount-board strips to inner surface of back rectangle, close to one short and two long edges, leaving free the one through which you will insert your photograph.

17 To join the front to the back, apply glue to spacers. With wrong sides together, place front over back, matching up all edges. Press together firmly. Allow to dry thoroughly.

18 While the frame is drying hold layers together with clothes pegs. To avoid leaving marks in the fabric, do not use clothes pegs for more than 30 minutes.

19 The frame can be hung on the wall by making a buttonhole loop on upper edge of back, using toning embroidery thread or a stand can be made as follows:

20 Using the stand board as a template, cut two tapered rectangles measuring 15 × 5 × 2.6cm/6 × 2 × 1¼in from main fabric, leaving an extra seam allowance of 1.5cm/½in all round.

21 Turn in a 0.75cm/¼in seam on the longer of the two short edges on both pieces of fabric and press.

22 With right sides together, pin stand covers together, making sure all edges are even. Stitch round a 1.5cm/½in seam, leaving pressed edges open to turn. Clip and trim corners, turn stand cover and press.

23 Score mount board along a solid line drawn 1.5cm/½in from upper narrow edge. Fold backwards and forwards to form a hinge.

24 Insert board through opening in stand cover. Slip stitch lower edge closed, using toning thread and tiny stitches.

25 Try standing the frame upright, using the stand to prop it in position. When you are satisfied that the stand is in the right place, mark the position lightly with a soft pencil. Glue stand flap to back of the picture frame, making sure that it sits within the pencil mark. Allow to dry flat, weighted down with heavy books.

26 Cut a length of ribbon 10cm/4in long approx. Try this piece of ribbon high up between the frame and the stand, in a position to stop the stand slipping open. When you are happy with its position glue one end to frame back and the other to the stand. Trim away any excess ribbon, if necessary.

27 You can now insert your favourite picture.

A selection of these frames looks extremely effective if produced in a variety of toning fabrics.

RAG RUG

RAG RUGS were extremely popular in the not-too-distant past. They were easy to make – the entire family could lend a hand – and the necessary materials were cheaply and readily available. In the days when the family income was spent on providing the necessities of life, a rag rug would lend a touch of comfort in an otherwise spartan room. In the coldest of the winter weather, a rag rug would also often have provided extra warmth on the children's bed.

Rag rugs are both decorative and hardwearing and contain a store of memories of garments, which otherwise would have outlived their usefulness. Such a rug can proudly take its place in today's cottage and will also blend happily into a more modern setting.

All types of rags can be used but lighter weights are best reserved for bedrooms and bathrooms where they will not be subjected to a great deal of wear and tear. Traditionally, most rags were used in their original state, which gives a more random effect, but more decorative effects can be obtained by dyeing them in a range of toning or contrasting colours.

MATERIALS

a rectangle of open-meshed hessian or sacking
strong sewing cotton
strong needle
PVA adhesive
old medium-weight clothes – jackets, suits, etc
a large crochet hook
or
rug-making latchet
hessian or canvas backing fabric

METHOD

1 Decide what size you want your finished rug to be and then, allowing an extra 5cm/2in all round, cut out hessian or sacking to this measurement.

2 Turn each edge over and hem, using strong cotton, to prevent fraying.

3 Cut up the old clothes into rags 2cm/½in wide and 5–8cm/2–3in long. The longer the strips, the deeper the finished pile will be.

4 Using a crochet or latchet hook, simply pull the rags through, one at a time, to form loops in the hessian. These can then be knotted with a simple knot or left loose. If the latter method is preferred, the back of the completed rug must be stuck firmly with a PVA glue to a hessian or canvas backing to prevent the rags working free.

5 Continue to pull the rags through the backing, keeping each row as close to the next as possible. The rags can be inserted at random, or can be grouped to produce a geometric pattern, as here.

6 When the rug is completed, turn in the 5cm/2in allowance. Turn in and tack a 5cm/2in seam allowance on the backing material. Spread adhesive on wrong side of rug, making sure not to work too close to the edges. Lay on the backing material and smooth flat to ensure a good bonding. When the adhesive is completely dry, slip stitch the two fabrics together along all edges, using strong thread in a toning colour making sure you finish off firmly to prevent the two layers from separating.

RAGS TO RICHES
*Recycle any spare pieces of fabric to make a
cheerful and unusual rag rug that will brighten
any hallway*

PRESSED FLOWER PICTURE

a selection of flower heads
a few sheets of blotting paper
heavy books or weights
or
a flower press
30 × 30cm/12 × 12in sheet of cartridge paper
HB lead pencil
ruler
a pair of compasses
or
20cm/8in diameter plate
all-purpose glue
30 × 30cm/12 × 12in coloured mounting card
with 26cm/10in circle cut out
30 × 30cm/12 × 12in frame

MEASUREMENTS

To make a picture measuring 30 × 30cm/12 × 12in

METHOD

1 Pick your chosen flower heads in the morning on a dry day, after the dew has evaporated. The best subjects for pressing are flat-faced flowers such as daisies, pansies, buttercups, etc. Also select a variety of leaves and ferns.

2 Place the flowers, leaves and ferns on to blotting paper, cover with another sheet of blotting paper and press between some heavy books, or boards loaded with weights. Take sufficient time to ensure that the flower heads, etc, lie flat. Many disappointments are caused by not laying out the subjects properly before pressing. A purchased flower press can, of course, be used. Leave undisturbed for at least four weeks.

3 After four weeks (or when the flowers are sufficiently pressed and completely dry), take your sheet of white cartridge paper and, measuring accurately, mark the centre of the sheet with a light pencil mark.

4 Take your compasses and using the centre mark, draw a circle with a diameter of 20cm/8in. Alternatively, centre the plate on the sheet of paper and, holding it firmly, draw carefully around it.

5 Place the smaller dried flower heads and leaves around the circle in a pleasing arrangement. When the design is to your satisfaction, carefully work around the circle, lifting each item and glueing lightly before pressing back into position.

6 To complete the picture, take the larger flowers, with a selection of leaves and ferns, and arrange a small bouquet in the centre of the circle. Lift and glue as before, taking care not to disturb the outer circle.

7 Leave to dry completely. Place the mount over the design, centring as accurately as possible. Secure in place with a little glue.

8 Frame and hang.

A family photograph, particularly an old one, looks effective if its mount is decorated with a small spray of dried flowers before framing (see jacket photograph).

FOLIAGE AND FLOWERS
Richly-patterned wallpaper provides a leafy
background to this pretty pressed flower design,
subtly illuminated by warm candlelight

CRAZY PATCHWORK CUSHION

IF SPACE PERMITS, a small chair looks inviting in the hall and provides a place for the visitor to leave coats and bags. The scraps left over from making fabric-covered picture frames can be utilised to make a co-ordinating cushion in the style of Victorian crazy patchwork. In this type of work, small irregular scraps are overlapped side by side and feather stitched into position, thus using up otherwise useless remnants. Pretty printed cottons and chintzes work well in crazy patchwork, but in our example velvet and silks have been worked together to give a more opulent look. For the best results always use fabrics of a similar weight and with similar properties.

MATERIALS

scraps left from fabric-covered frames
or
a good selection of toning or contrasting velvet and heavyweight silk fabrics
0.5m/½yd of 90cm/36in calico for backing
reel of tacking cotton
sewing needles
3 skeins of toning embroidery thread
embroidery needles
1 reel of sewing cotton in toning colour
fabric marker pen (optional)
36cm/14in velcro
36cm/14in cushion pad

MEASUREMENTS

Finished measurement is 36 × 36cm/14 × 14in

METHOD

1 Assemble all your scraps and lay them out roughly to give a good mix of patterns and colour. The scraps can be of varying sizes and shapes, but the edges should be made up of straight lines.
2 From the calico cut two squares measuring 40 × 40cm/16 × 16in.

3 Turn in and tack the edges on a selection of scraps. Crazy patchwork can be started either from one corner or from the central scrap. Our example was worked from the central point outwards, overlapping each scrap slightly with its neighbour. Start tacking fabric scraps on to one square of calico in a random fashion.
4 Work in this manner until all the calico is covered.
5 Using feather stitch (see diagram) and three strands of embroidery thread, work over all joins to anchor down scraps.
6 Remove tacking threads and press.
7 Repeat the above instructions on second square of calico.
8 Place right sides of work together and machine stitch around three sides, leaving a 2.5cm/1in seam allowance. Trim seam allowance to 1.25cm/½in. Cut off across corners fairly close to stitching. Turn and press.
9 Turn in seam allowance on raw edges and press firmly. Tack velcro into position along these seam lines. Check that it will lie flat when completed, and machine stitch into position.
10 Remove tacking stitches, press cushion cover and insert cushion pad.

Crazy patchwork can be further embellished by embroidering initials and the date on one patch. Just sign your name and the date on one patch of the completed square before assembly using a fabric marker pen, and then embroider using a darker or contrasting shade of embroidery thread and stem stitch (see diagram). Family names, anniversary dates and so on could also be added. The more heavily embroidered the patchwork becomes, the more authentic it will appear.

Feather stitch   *Stem stitch*

A CRAZY CUSHION
Scraps of velvet and silk in contrasting shades
have been combined through the use of feather
stitch to make an eye-catching patchwork
cushion

23

CHAPTER 2
THE KITCHEN

THE KITCHEN SHOULD BE the warm and welcoming heart of the house – a place for family and friends to unwind after the struggles of the day. On a cold winter's afternoon, in the perfect kitchen, a cheerful log fire burns in the hearth, the smell of freshly baked bread fills the air and a pan of homemade soup simmers on the stove. All around are homely examples of skill and ingenuity – personal additions that add to the inviting atmosphere and provide focal points.

If space permits the kitchen is the ideal setting for informal family dinners during the week and, cosily decorated, it can be a room for entertaining weekend guests, while the cook is busily preparing a meal.

The kitchen of today is vastly different from the country-cottage kitchen of the past. Fitted kitchens, the inspiration of the Bauhaus movement in the early 1900s, revolutionised our furnishing of this very important room. Today, scrubbed pine or light oak is the obvious choice to create the right ambience. The display of a treasured collection of old tins, teapots or plates will help to generate the feeling of warmth and welcome, and armfuls of dried flowers or bunches of dried herbs will reinforce this country theme.

When planning craft items for the country kitchen, let your imagination run riot. A well-planned miscellany of personally-produced artefacts will add charm and character and turn your kitchen into the room you always dreamed of owning.

THE COUNTRY KITCHEN
*Fresh green foliage, scented flowers and warm,
new-baked bread – country life at its very best*

BARGE ART COAL-SCUTTLE

THE BEAUTY OF BARGE ART is its primitive peasant quality, which has been used for many years to decorate a variety of household items. It is an art which has been popular for about two hundred years, developing with the growth of the canal network across Europe. Its simplicity of style does not take a great measure of artistic ability to reproduce and it is, therefore, within the range of most people. It is a source of great satisfaction to even the least artistic of us to be able to produce an item of which to be proud, especially from an old and battered coal-scuttle!

Variations in barge art design can be attributed to regional styles and, of course, individual artists developed their own particular style. However, one strict rule did evolve, which governed the design and colour used for each part of the boat and its accessories. Any colour can be used for the background, but traditionally, the artist would have chosen from dark blue, dark red, dark green or black.

It is a matter of personal preference whether you follow the design given here, or draw your own flowers directly on to the scuttle. Whichever design you choose, the method of working will be the same.

MATERIALS

1 new or well-cleaned upright coal-scuttle
wire wool
newspaper
1 can dark green car spray-paint
tracing paper
soft white pencil
masking tape
2H lead pencils
selection of enamel paints (tiny tins for model making)
1 medium artist's paintbrush

METHOD

1 If you are using an old coal-scuttle, make sure that it is scrupulously clean by rubbing over thoroughly with wire wool. Wash to remove dust and dirt and leave until completely dry.

2 Stand the coal scuttle on sheets of newspaper and spray an even coat of paint all over it. It is best to do this outside on a fairly still, dry day. The scuttle will need at least two coats of paint, but one can of spray paint should be sufficient.

3 Following the diagrams on pages 28–9, trace the bouquets on to the tracing paper, using a sharp, soft white pencil.

4 Turn the tracing paper over and secure in place on the coal-scuttle with masking tape. Using a sharp, hard lead pencil draw over the design quite firmly. Remove the paper. The design should be just visible on the scuttle. If you are drawing your own design freehand, just use the soft white pencil to draw directly on to the coal-scuttle.

5 Now using the enamel paints and a medium-sized brush, start to paint in the designs, decorating the edgings and handles as you feel appropriate.

This form of decoration need not be restricted to coal-scuttles, any simple household items can be painted in this way: watering cans, kitchen scales, enamel jugs or even wooden boxes, spoons or chairs. Use your imagination to create delightful and unique works of art!

THE KITCHEN RANGE
An old black coal-scuttle, brightly painted with
a traditional barge art design, is a decorative
and useful addition to the country kitchen

CARE OF YOUR FINISHED BARGE ART

1 Do not use metal scouring pads or harsh abrasive cleaners.
2 Keep away from sources of direct heat, such as open fires, hot radiators, etc.
3 Wash carefully with a damp sponge and warm soapy water. Then polish dry with a soft clean cloth.
4 The painted finish is liable to chip, so treat carefully.

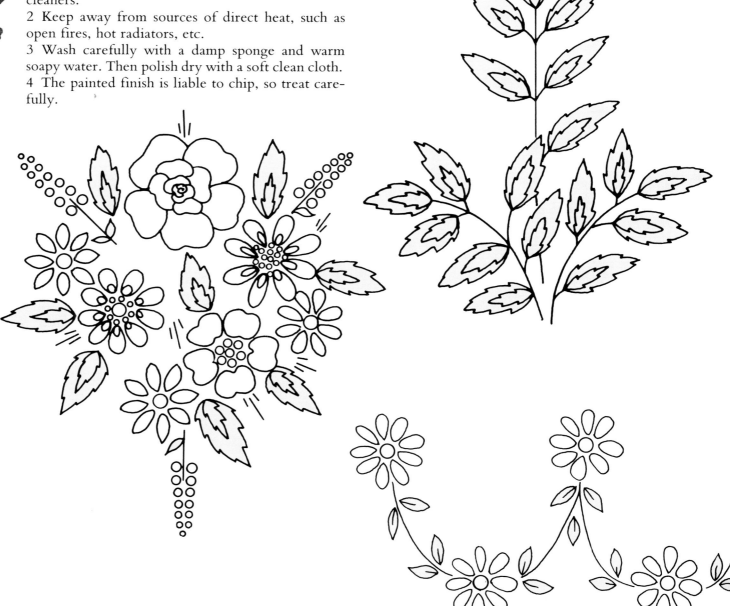

WOVEN CANE BASKET

A BASKET CAN BE MADE from a variety of different canes: willow, bramble, hazel, elm. If you decide to collect these canes yourself, rather than purchasing them from a specialist shop, you will need to select straight, one-year-old twigs – the ones with no side shoots. They must be pliable enough to plait and weave. So, to test this, wind them around your wrist. Reject any which crack or do not bend easily.

The best time to gather twigs is during the winter, from November to March. Remember not to strip all your twigs from just one bush: take a few choice twigs from each plant, selecting with care. In order not to damage the tree by pulling away the twigs use sharp secateurs or a pruning knife, making sure the cut is as clean as possible.

A word of warning – it is wise, and polite, to ask permission from the landowner first. Also, do not make the mistake of weakening hedges around fields. This might result in livestock straying on to the road and could cause accidents.

You can, of course, look to your own garden for suitable materials. Many garden climbers can be used; try experimenting with a selection of varieties to find the most suitable.

Having followed all the rules and equipped yourself with a good-sized bundle of twigs, you are now ready to attempt your first basket.

MATERIALS

a large bundle of twigs
bramble, clematis, elm, ivy, hazel, privet or sloe
a ball of medium thickness string
a bowl or bucket for soaking the canes
damp cloth
sharp knife or secateurs

PREPARATION

Unless your twigs are of bramble or elm, it will be necessary to prepare them for working. This process is known as 'fading' and is performed to dry the twigs, whilst still keeping them pliable.

1 Keeping each variety of twigs separate, tie them into bundles and leave them outside in a sheltered position for a period of time (ranging from two weeks to three months). This time depends on the thickness of the twigs and the type of wood used. During the 'fading' time, do keep checking them. They must not become too dry or they will be brittle and unworkable. They are ready when the sticks feel leathery. If, by mischance, you feel they have become too dry, soak them in a bucket of water for two days. After this time they should be left out for another day and then wrapped in a damp cloth until you are ready to work them.

2 Now sort out the sticks and put them into bundles, according to type and thickness. The thickness of the sticks will determine their use.

Bottom or Base Sticks
The thickest, shortest sticks are used to make the foundation of the basket.

Side Stakes
The side stakes should be made from sticks of medium thickness, cut to a length some 20cm/8in longer than the height of the completed basket (in this case 43cm/17in long).

Weavers
The weavers should be the thinnest and most pliable twigs. In order to make your work easier, try to make these as long as possible.

3 The twigs must be damp to enable them to be more easily worked, so soak each bundle in water for an hour before starting to make your basket.

METHOD

1 Take 8 thick bottom sticks (about 25–30cm/10–12in long) and slit 4 through the middle, then push the other 4 sticks through these slits (diagram 1).

2 Select a long weaving twig and loop it over one bundle of bottom sticks about halfway down its

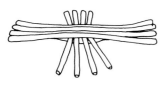

Diagram 1

length. Take the two ends around each bundle (diagram 2).

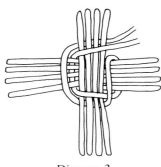

Diagram 2

3 Now fan out the bottom sticks to form an even circle and start to weave in and out (diagram 3) until the base measures approximately 20cm/8in.

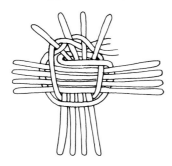

Diagram 3

4 Cut off the excess length of the bottom sticks with a sharp knife.

5 Take 10 side sticks, approximately 43cm/17in long, and taper one end of each of them with a sharp knife. Push this pointed end into the woven base at the side of a bottom stick.

6 Bend up the side stakes to form the skeleton of the basket and tie in position with a piece of string (diagram 4).

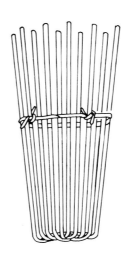

Diagram 4

7 Take 3 medium thickness twigs and place each one behind 3 consecutive side stakes. Weave them around the sides of the basket, but taking each twig around 2 side stakes at a time. Continue weaving until 3 rounds have been completed (diagram 5).

Diagram 5

8 Now select your weavers for the main body of the basket. Each one must be at least 2.5cm/1in longer than the circumference of the basket (in this case 89cm + 2.5cm/35in + 1in).

9 Take the thickest end of the weaver and put it

31

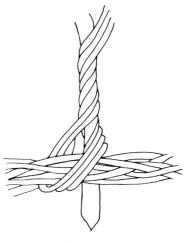

behind a side stake. Weave in front and behind each side stake until the end is reached. Finish off by tucking the end behind a side stake.

10 To join a new weaver, just tuck the thickest end behind the same stake and continue to weave.

11 Continue weaving in this way until the height of the basket measures 19cm/7½in, alternating the weaving pattern as shown on the fourth and then every third round (diagram 6).

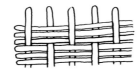

Diagram 6

Diagram 8

12 Complete the basket side with 3 rounds, as described in step 7.

13 To finish off the basket, bend and weave the side stakes as shown in diagram 7. This is known as a 'trac' border and needs only 5cm/2in of side stakes. If necessary, trim off the excess with a sharp knife before starting the border.

The above instructions can be followed using willow canes which can be purchased from good craft supply shops or by mail order from W. Gadsby & Son (Burrowbridge) Ltd, Burrowbridge Basket Works, Burrowbridge, Bridgwater, Somerset.

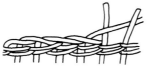

Diagram 7

14 To form the handle, take a good thick bottom stick (about 82cm/32in long) and sharpen each end. Push each end well down through the border and into the body of the basket (about 15–18cm/6–7in).

15 Take 3 thin weavers, loop through the border and bind over the handle rod to the other side. Push the ends into the top of the border and bind and plait as shown in diagram 8, using 5 thin weaving twigs on either side. Finish off neatly by pushing the ends into the border.

GOLDEN RULES
A neat kitchen sampler reminds the conscientious cook of her duties, while a woven cane basket bursting with fresh garden produce awaits her attention

Golden Rules for the Kitchen

A good cook wastes nothing

Haste without hurry saves
worry, fuss, and flurry

Soup boiled is soup spoiled

An hour lost in the morning
has to be run after all day

SAMPLER

MIDDLE-CLASS VICTORIANS believed that cleanliness, thrift and order were of paramount importance in the kitchen and the popular books of household management of the day suggested that homely maxims should be written out and displayed – a constant reminder, no doubt (should it be needed!), to the cook. It was often (surprisingly) recommended that these texts might include an ornamental border to embellish and improve the kitchen, and we have kept this recommendation in mind whilst designing this sampler for our country cottage kitchen.

You can, of course, adapt this idea to a theme of your own choosing and so a chart of letters is provided for your guidance. When planning your own sampler, draw out these letters on to graph paper before starting to embroider, making sure that each line is correctly placed and balanced.

The sampler shown on page 33 carries the following Victorian advice:

Golden Rules for the Kitchen

A good cook wastes nothing

*Haste without hurry, saves
worry, fuss and flurry*

Soup boiled is soup spoiled

*An hour lost in the morning
has to be run after all day*

MATERIALS

*41 × 41cm/16 × 16in square of cream evenweave material
(22 threads to 2.5cm/1in)
dark tacking cotton
sharps needle
Twilleys Lystra stranded embroidery cotton:
2 skeins of 43 – medium green
1 skein each of
30 – mustard
29 – mushroom
28 – medium brown
fine crewel needle
a piece of heavy white card, measuring 35.5 × 46cm/14 × 18in
heavy-duty linen or cotton thread
a piece of mounting card, measuring 35.5 × 46cm/14 × 18in,
with a window measuring 23 × 29.5cm/9 × 11½in
dark-wood frame measuring 35.5 × 46cm/14 × 18in*

MEASUREMENTS

Finished picture measures 35.5 × 46cm/14 × 18in

METHOD

1 Press the material flat, fold in half lengthways and press, then fold crossways and press. Using long tacking stitches and a scrap of dark cotton, mark these ironed-in centre lines.

2 Turn over 1.25cm/½in all around and hem the fabric to prevent fraying.

3 Following the chart, start by working the heading **Golden Rules for the Kitchen**. To find the starting point, measure 10cm/4in down from the top edge of the fabric along the centre line of tacking and then work from this centre line outwards. This will ensure that the sampler lies centrally on the fabric. You can then use the heading as a guide for placing the rest of the lettering. Embroider the sampler using cross stitch for the edging pattern and back stitch for all lettering (see diagrams).

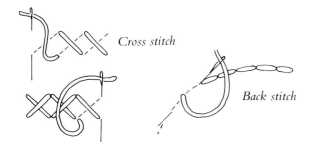

Cross stitch

Back stitch

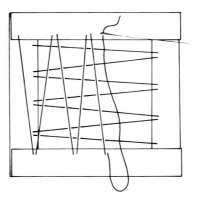

4 When the design is complete wash the sampler, if necessary, and leave to dry. When almost dry, press thoroughly on the reverse side using a hot steam iron.
5 Now, taking a rectangle of mounting card, centre the sampler over the white side and turn the edges over the edges of the card. Using strong thread, doubled and knotted, work backwards and forwards across the back of the sampler, pulling the fabric quite tightly with each stitch (see diagram). Work the long edges first and then the short edges and continue until all the edges are firmly stretched and held.

Mounting the sampler

The sampler in our kitchen was then mounted behind a dark-green mounting card and framed in a narrow dark-wood frame, to give an authentic touch.

It is possible to find excellent old wooden frames in bric-à-brac shops at exceedingly reasonable prices. Do, however, check for woodworm before making your purchase.

SUFFOLK STAR PATCHWORK TEAPOT STAND

THIS HIGHLY DECORATIVE form of patchwork is simple and quick to do and has been used here to make an unusual teapot stand. The heat of the freshly filled pot will draw out the fragrance of the spices, which will remain strong for many months and can be replaced time and time again.

MATERIALS

piece of calico measuring 25 × 25cm/10 × 10in
HB pencil
ruler
piece of stiff card
pair of compasses
scalpel
metal ruler
scraps of printed cotton material in toning colours
sharp scissors
white sewing thread
sharps needles
saucer or small plate
dressmaker's pins
piece of muslin 25 × 50cm/10 × 20in
piece of medium-weight wadding 25 × 50cm/10 × 20in
selection of whole sweet spices

MEASUREMENTS

The finished teapot stand has a diameter of 13cm/7in

METHOD

1 Fold the piece of calico in half and press firmly with a warm iron.
2 Open out, turn a quarter turn, fold and press again. It is necessary to do this accurately to give the centre of the fabric.
3 Using a soft lead pencil and a ruler, draw in these lines.
4 Now fold from corner to corner. Press. Using the ruler, draw in a line through this crease and the centre point, taking the line to the edges of the fabric.
5 Fold from opposite corners and repeat step 4 (diagram 1).

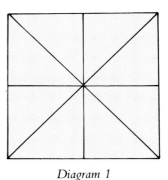

Diagram 1

6 Using a ruler and compasses draw an 8cm/3in square on the piece of card as follows:
a) Draw a line (approx 23cm/9in) and mark the centre point A (diagram 2).
b) Open the compasses to 8cm/3in and put the compass point on point A and make two further marks on the line each side of the original (diagram 3).

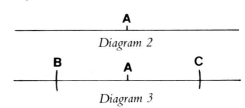

Diagram 2

Diagram 3

c) Extend the compasses slightly, put the compass point on to mark B and draw an arc above the line, above point A (diagram 4, overleaf).

THE SUMMER KITCHEN
Early morning sunlight picks up the fresh greens and toning shades of an unusual spice-filled, patchwork teapot stand, surrounded by a selection of herbs picked ready for drying. An aromatic clove orange hangs from the spice rack

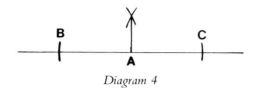

Diagram 4

d) Move compasses to mark C and repeat, crossing the first arc (diagram 4).

e) Draw a line from the crossing of the arcs to point A. This gives you a right angle (diagram 4).

f) Open the compasses to 8cm/3in again. Place point of compass on point A and bisect the vertical line (diagram 5).

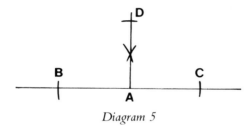

Diagram 5

g) Move compasses to mark D and draw an arc parallel to the base line (diagram 6).

h) Move compasses to point E and draw an arc which bisects the last arc (diagram 6).

i) With a ruler, draw a line between D and the point where the arcs cross and another line from E to the point where the arcs cross (diagram 6).

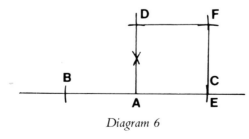

Diagram 6

Using a scalpel and metal ruler, cut out the square thus formed, which will be used as a template for drawing your patchwork squares.

7 Press all your scraps of material flat and decide which you will use to form the centre of your star. Using your template draw round and cut out four squares in this fabric (a).

8 Fold each square in half carefully and press.

9 Now fold folded edges together down the centre line (diagram 7) and press firmly.

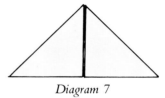

Diagram 7

10 These patches are now ready to be sewn in position on the calico. Make sure that the points fit snugly together and that the fold lines lie on the original crease lines in the calico. Stitch cut edges down firmly by hand or machine, making sure to keep stitches as near to edge as possible.

11 Cut eight 8cm/3in squares from the next scrap of cotton (b). Fold and press as before and position along drawn lines as shown in diagram 8, making sure that the stitches of the previous row are completely covered.

12 Cut eight squares in third (c) and fourth (d) scraps

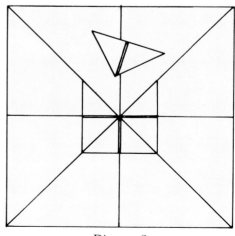

Diagram 8

of cotton, fold, press and position as before, making sure the previous row of stitching is covered.

13 Finally, finish with a fifth circle of patches in fabric (a), cutting, folding and pressing as before and positioning each row over last as shown in diagram 9.

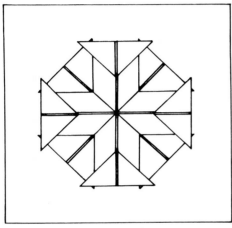

Diagram 9

Stitch down firmly and trim off excess calico.

14 Catch down the point of each triangle with a few oversewing stitches.

15 Draw out a circle, with a radius of 13cm/7in on to fabric (a) and cut out. Put patchwork piece and fabric circle right sides together, tack and stitch, leaving a small opening sufficient to turn right side out.

16 Using a saucer, or small plate, draw two circles on muslin and cut out. Pin muslin to wadding and cut out two wadding circles.

17 Place two pieces of muslin and wadding together and stitch, muslin sides out, leaving a small gap for filling. Fill with a selection of sweet spices, such as star anise, cinnamon bark, allspice. Sew up opening very firmly. Do not fill too full or the teapot will not sit firmly on the finished cushion.

18 Put this pad inside the patchwork cover, turn in raw edges and slip stitch together. Do not stitch too tightly, as these stitches will need to be unpicked from time to time to enable the cover to be washed.

CLOVE ORANGE

CLOVE ORANGES were originally made in medieval times to prevent the spread of infection and to sweeten the air. Properly made, their delightful fragrance will last for many years and will provide a decorative addition to the country kitchen.

MATERIALS

skewer or bodkin
25–50g/1–2oz cloves
thin-skinned Seville oranges (available in January and February)
for each orange allow:
100g/4oz ground orris root
5ml/1tspn ground cinnamon
tissue paper
approx 1m/1yd of 1.25cm/½in velvet ribbon
scraps of lace
long steel pins or heavy-duty staples

METHOD

1 Using a skewer or bodkin to make the holes, push the cloves into the orange in circles, starting from the stalk end. Leave a little space between each clove, as the orange will shrink as it dries.

2 When the orange is completely covered, roll it in the orris root powder, mixed with the cinnamon. Push the mixture well into the cloves, but try not to break the heads from their stalks.

3 When as much spice mixture has been used as possible, wrap the orange in white tissue paper and put into a drawer to season for at least six weeks.

4 At the end of this time, remove the tissue paper and brush the orange carefully to remove excess powder. Again, be careful not to dislodge the cloves.

5 Now decorate with velvet ribbons and lace, finishing by forming a loop in the ribbon, to enable the orange to be hung over a hook in the kitchen or in a wardrobe to sweeten your linen and deter moths. The ribbons can be secured with long steel pins or heavy-duty staples.

39

BOUQUET GARNI OR BUNDLE OF HERBS

A TRADITIONAL FEATURE of the country kitchen in summer has always been the huge bunches of herbs and flowers, hung in a corner to dry. The modern method of freezing herbs for use in the winter months, whilst being a very valid alternative, does not have the charm of the dried variety and, if quantity permits, a few bundles of herbs can be hung from a beam in the kitchen to remain there throughout the winter to remind the cook of the hot summer morning on which they were picked.

A traditional all-purpose herb mix for bouquet garni is parsley, thyme and marjoram, together with a bay leaf, but the mixture can be varied according to the dish in which it is to be used.

MATERIALS

0.25m/¼yd of fine natural muslin
sharp scissors
selection of dried herbs including dried bay leaves
cream sewing cotton
light-proof and airtight jar or jars

METHOD

1 Cut out small squares from the muslin (about 8cm/3in square).
2 Put a teaspoon of mixed dried herbs and a dried bay leaf into the centre of each square.
3 Draw up the edges over the herbs to form a small bag. Tie the neck tightly with a length of sewing cotton and knot securely.
4 Store in light-proof, airtight jars in a cool dry place.

POEM PICTURE

A POEM CONCERNED with a typically English recipe has been used to make our picture. You do not need to use a poem: an old family saying or recipe could be treated in the same way to make a very personal heirloom. This particular picture was made with a piece of old bobbin lace rescued from a torn handkerchief, but a narrow strip of machine-made leaver's lace could be used, or a crochet edging, purchased braid, or even broderie anglaise – anything decorative, in fact, which takes your eye.

A good source of scraps of haberdashery are the rummage boxes at antique and collectors' fairs. Very often short lengths of beautiful edgings can be rescued for small sums of money and these can be given a new lease of life. The only limitation is your imagination!

MATERIALS

HB lead pencil
ruler
sheet of heavy white cartridge paper 25 × 25cm/10 × 10in
a sheet of dry rub-down lettering in suitable type face
or
calligraphy pen and gold ink
a sheet of dark blue mounting card 30.5 × 30.5cm/12 × 12in
with a rectangular window 18 × 11.5 cm/7 × 4½in
rectangle of 5cm/2in wide handmade lace approx
21.25 × 15cm/8½ × 6in (this measurement variable according
to individual taste)

AN EIGHTEENTH-CENTURY ADAGE
This charming verse exhorts the cook to greater efforts in her quest for perfect pastry – prettily surrounded by antique lace and posies of flowers

"Dear Nelly! learn with care the pastry art,
And mind the easy precepts I impart:
Draw out your dough elaborately thin,
And cease not to fatigue your rolling pin:
Of eggs and butter see you mix enough,
For then the paste will swell into a puff,
Which will in crumpling sounds your praise report,
And eat, as housewives speak, exceeding short."

King.

or
approx 112.5 × 5cm/44 × 2in wide crocheted, knitted or purchased edging
heavy-duty fungicide wallpaper paste for mounting lace or braid
fine paintbrush
a few pressed flower heads and small leaves
suitable wooden frame measuring 30.5 × 30.5cm/12 × 12in, preferably with a little gold decoration

MEASUREMENTS

The finished size of the picture shown here is 30.5 × 30.5cm/ 12 × 12in

The poem chosen is an old one concerned with the making of light pastry – as important now as when it was written in the eighteenth century!

> *Dear Nelly! learn with care the pastry art,*
> *And mind the easy precepts I impart:*
> *Draw out your dough, elaborately thin,*
> *And cease not to fatigue your rolling pin:*
> *Of eggs and butter see you mix enough,*
> *For then the paste will swell into a puff,*
> *What will in crumpling sounds your praise report*
> *And eat, as housewives speak, exceedingly short.*
>
> King

METHOD

1 Using a newly sharpened HB lead pencil and ruler carefully measure and mark the centre of the paper, drawing a line across from edge to edge.
2 Measure either side of this line, and mark off the correct number of lines to give a guide for lettering.
3 Write out the poem or apply lettering according to instructions printed on the sheet, making sure to judge the distance between each letter accurately.
4 Measure in 1.25cm/½in from outer edge of mount and draw a fine line all around edge as a guide for attaching border. This measurement will obviously vary according to the size of your piece of lace, the

size of the mount, window, etc. In which case, place the lace on the mount in the most pleasing way, measure its distance from the edge of the mount and draw the guide line accordingly.
5 Using heavy-duty wallpaper paste, make up sufficient to attach lace or braid to the mount. 5ml/1tsp of paste to 15ml/3tsps of water should be sufficient. The paste should be fairly thick. Wallpaper paste will hold the lace and dries almost completely invisibly. It also has the advantage of being water soluble and will wash out completely if necessary.
6 Using a very clean, fine paintbrush, apply paste to wrong side of lace or braid, etc, and stick in position very carefully. Leave to dry for at least four hours.
7 If you are using your own handmade lace there is no need to sew in ends. These can now be threaded through a strong needle and drawn through the mount to lie at the back of the work.
8 Now, use the pressed flowers and leaves to make a little bouquet over the join line of the border. When you are happy with your arrangement lift each flower, apply a little wallpaper paste and replace. Alternatively, make little bouquets of pressed flowers and arrange between the poem and the lace.
9 Leave for 24 hours before mounting and framing.

If the lace you have used is very precious, it is advisable to get expert advice on framing. The glass should not come into contact with the fabric and acid-free paper should be used. In some cases, it is advisable to use special glass when displaying lace and advice can usually be obtained from the keeper of textiles at any large museum.

A final word: if you intend to use old lace it is always advisable to seek advice from an expert before cutting it up for whatever purpose. Old lace is often a beautiful and precious material and should be treated with respect. That said, there are many scraps of old torchon and Bedfordshire lace which deserve to be given a new lease of life and, used in this way, will give a great deal of pleasure for many years to come.

DRIED FLOWER DECORATED BASKET

MATERIALS

a selection of small dried flowers
choose from:
Ammobium alatum *(sand flower)*
Catananche caerulea *(cupid's dart)*
Helichrysum bracteatum *(straw daisy)*
ornamental grasses
tiny poppy seed heads
Rhodanthe manglesii
tiny rosebuds
Limonium sinuatum *(statice)*
florists' wire
scissors
a pretty woven basket
pliers
essential oils (optional)

METHOD

1 Make the dried flowers up into tiny bunches and trim stems to about 8cm/3in long. These look better if individually bunched, but you could try making little mixed bunches if you wished.

2 Cut lengths of florists' wire, approximately 10–15cm/4–6in long, depending upon the thickness of the walls of your basket.

3 Wind the wire tightly around each bunch of flowers and then push the wire ends through the rim of the basket.

4 Using the pliers, twist the wire round tightly to secure flowers upright on outer rim and trim off ends of wire, pushing ends back along inner rim.

5 Continue around the whole rim of basket, placing each bunch close to its neighbours and alternating flower types at random.

6 Small bunches of flowers can also be secured in the same way over the handle of the basket, using each following bunch to hide the wire securing the previous one.

Hung from a hook in the kitchen or in the sitting-room, these baskets will remain lovely for many years. A few drops of essential oils, such as rose or lavender can be dropped on to the flowers from time to time.

CROCHET KITCHEN TEA-COSY

THE IDEA FOR this tea-cosy was taken from a small Edwardian example, found at a local jumble sale. The ribbed texture is achieved by using a raised treble stitch and the colours used are as close as possible to the original.

MATERIALS

1 ball Twilleys Stalite perlespun mercerised cotton No 3
in the following colours:
21 – cream
106 – light beige
22 – medium beige
68 – lemon
109 – pale pink
58 – medium pink
30 – dusky pink
115 – pearl grey
57 – light fuchsia
27 – gold
no 2 crochet hook

ABBREVIATIONS

st – stitch
sts – stitches
ch – chain
dc – double crochet [single crochet]*
tr – treble [double crochet]
h tr – half treble [half double crochet]
dbl tr – double treble [treble]
yrh – yarn round hook
rtf – raised treble forward [raised double crochet forward]
*[USA equivalents]

MEASUREMENTS

The finished tea-cosy will fit an average sized teapot and was made for a traditional brown kitchen pot. Its size can be varied by reducing or increasing the number of stitches on each panel.

METHOD

1 Using no 30 – dusky rose – make a chain of 80 sts (including 3 turning ch).

2 Miss 3 ch and make a foundation row of 1 tr into each ch (77 tr). 1 turning ch. Turn work.

3 1 dc into each tr to end, 1 dc into turning ch, 2 ch turn.

4 Change to no 21 – cream – * yrh, keeping hook at front of work, insert hook from right to left round stem of next tr on foundation and work a tr (rtf), miss dc above this tr, 1 dc into next dc, rep from * to end, ending with 1 rtf round stem of least tr, 1 dc into turning ch, 1 ch turn.

5 1 dc into each st to end, 1 dc into turning ch, 2 ch turn.

6 Change to no 22 – medium beige – * 1 rtf round stem of rtf on row 2, 1 dc into next dc, rep from * to end, working last dc into turning ch, 1 ch turn.

7 Rep row 5.

8 Rep rows 6 and 7, changing colour with each rep as follows: 27 – gold, 109 – pale pink, 115 – pearl grey, 68 – lemon, 106 – light beige, 57 – light fuchsia.

9 After 2 rows of light fuchsia, continue with 2 rows of dusky pink and rep complete colour sequence once more.

10 Fasten off and rep steps 1–9.

11 Rep row 6 using cream yarn and crochet across both pieces of work.

12 Do not turn work but continue to work around both pieces of work, thus forming a circle. Dc into each st of previous row.

13 Decrease on next row by missing 1 dc in every 4 dc.

14 Continue working round circle 6 times, decreasing as before.

15 Work round circle in dbl trs.

16 Work 3 rounds of dc into each st. Fasten off.

17 Make a cord by working 60 ch sts in medium beige and fasten off.

18 Make a flower by making a ring of 6 ch. Into ring

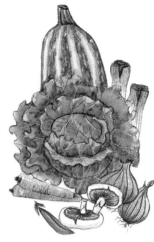

work * 1 dc, 1 h tr, 2 tr, 1 h tr, 1 dc, rep 3 times.
Fasten off. Repeat.

19 Sew up side seams, leaving gaps for handle and
spout. Thread cord through row of trs on cosy and
sew a flower to each cord end. Pull cord tight and finish with a bow.

THE TRADITIONAL ENGLISH TEATIME
*A good book, a slice of rich chocolate cake and
a refreshing cup of tea, kept hot with a pretty
crocheted tea-cosy in soft shades of pink and
cream*

CHAPTER 3
THE SITTING-ROOM

THE SITTING-ROOM is where most people spend time while relaxing. A great deal of thought should be given, therefore, to the decoration of this room. The craftswoman of today can use her skills to the greatest effect here, emulating her Victorian predecessors by making cushions, embroidered pictures, tablecloths – the list is almost endless.

Needlepoint is the traditional and practical choice for rugs, cushions, fire-screens and chair seats, while a cross stitch motto above the fireplace was (in bygone days) an almost obligatory furnishing accessory.

Windows can be dressed simply or given the full 'Victorian' treatment, with frilled pelmets, swags and valances of all descriptions.

The charm of this room is, however, mainly seen in attention to detail. The choice of cushions, pictures and ornaments help reinforce the mood of relaxation and enjoyment.

Use the sitting-room to display your most precious items – an invitation to the guest to browse and admire and a talking point for many conversations. It is here that your personality can really blossom, so do take time and plan your room for the maximum effect.

THE HEART OF THE HOME
*A perfect complement to the welcoming glow of
a real fire: an exquisite Victorian-style
firescreen, with work in progress*

NEEDLEPOINT FIRE-SCREEN

TENT STITCH HAS been one of the most widely used stitches for counted thread work since the sixteenth century. It was probably in use before this date, but in Tudor times professional needleworkers produced wall-hangings, carpets, chairs and sofas. Since these times, tent stitch or needlepoint has remained constantly popular and is used here to produce a Victorian-style fire-screen and matching fire-side rug.

MATERIALS

tapestry canvas 69 × 76cm/27 × 30in
masking tape
strong sewing cotton
marker pen
tapestry frame
Twilleys SEW Tapestry wools:
6 skeins each of the following colours
117 – mushroom   ×
116 – light mushroom   \
119 – dusky pink   +
120 – burgundy   ●
70 – light mint green   /
37 – dusky blue   —
tapestry needle
sharps needle
piece of cork board
blotting paper or white cotton or linen cloth
graph paper
drawing-pins

MEASUREMENTS

The finished measurement is approx 61 × 61cm/24 × 24in

The canvas used here has a thread count of 14 per inch. The size of the finished tapestry can be altered by changing the thread count. Divide the thread count per inch of the canvas into the chart thread count and then allow at least 7.5cm/3in on all four sides for stretching and mounting. This will give you the amount of canvas required.

METHOD

1 Prepare the canvas by binding the edges with masking tape, or by turning over and hemming 1.5cm/½in all round. This hem can then be tacked down using long running stitches.
2 Find the centre of the canvas by counting the number of threads across the width and divide by two. Using this figure, count this number of threads in towards the centre and mark with a marker pen. Do the same to find the centre of the length of the canvas. Using long running threads of sewing cotton, mark these lines across and down the canvas. These lines will give you points of reference with the chart, while working your design.
3 If using a frame, stitch the top and bottom of the canvas to the tape on the top and bottom bars of the frame and, if necessary, roll the canvas round until it is taut. For extra firmness a thread can be passed back and forth along each side of the canvas around the side bars. This thread should be pulled tight and finished off securely.
4 Follow the chart and colour guide to work the design as shown, using tent stitch for the design and basketweave stitch for any large areas of colour.
5 If working on recommended canvas size, use three strands of tapestry wool, but always separate the strands and put them back together before use, smoothing them together, before beginning to work. This will result in a better stitch texture: the stitches will lie more evenly and the threads will appear fuller. Do not use too much thread at one time and stop from time to time and let the needle hang freely to remove any twists put on the thread during working.
6 To begin work, put a knot in the end of the yarn and insert needle from the right side through to the back about 8cm/3in from the starting point. In this

case, above the middle point of the lower edge (115 threads down from the centre point of the canvas). Bring the needle back to the front of the work at this starting point and work the first row. Leave the knot until the rows of stitching are very close and then snip off close to canvas with sharp scissors. The thread on the other side will have been firmly secured by the stitches worked over it.

7 When joining or finishing threads, run under previously worked stitches at the back of the work and then snip off excess thread. If you leave long tails of thread on the reverse of your work the finished and stretched tapestry will have a lumpy appearance.

8 When the needlepoint chart is completed, take a piece of cork larger than the canvas and cover it with a sheet of blotting paper or a white cotton or linen cloth. Place a sheet of graph paper on top of this and pin down securely with drawing-pins. Place the finished tapestry face down on the graph paper and, using rustproof drawing-pins, secure one edge to the cork board. Use the line of the graph paper to ensure that the canvas is straight, pulling it into position as you work. Now pull and pin the opposite edge, damping the tapestry if necessary. Continue in the same manner around the other two edges. You may find that the third and fourth edges are more difficult, so pull a little harder to make sure it is all in line with the graph-paper lines.

9 Leave your work pinned to the cork board until it is completely dry. This may take several weeks, according to the temperature and the amount of water used to dampen the tapestry whilst stretching. Do be patient, to hurry this procedure could result in disappointment. The canvas should be left to dry naturally, do not be tempted to put it in front of a fire or in the oven!

10 Remove the pins and admire your handiwork. If you are not completely satisfied with the result, be strong willed and repeat the process until the tapestry is perfectly square.

11 The canvas is now ready to be mounted and made into your fire-screen.

DIAGRAMS FOR TENT STITCH

Diagrams are given for working tent stitch from a) right to left, b) left to right, c) down, d) up.

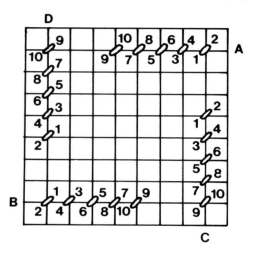

DIAGRAM FOR BASKETWEAVE STITCH

This stitch, used for larger blocks of colour, will help prevent distortion of the work. Always work in diagonal rows up and down.

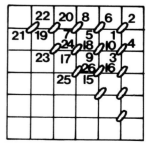

NEEDLEPOINT FIRESIDE RUG

MATERIALS

tapestry canvas 135 × 76cm/54 × 30in
Twilleys SEW Tapestry wools: 12 skeins each of the colours used
for the needlepoint fire-screen (page 48)
size 14 tapestry needle
backing fabric 125 × 65cm/50 × 26in
strong thread
natural cotton for fringing

MEASUREMENTS

The finished size of the rug is 120 × 60cm/48 × 24in

METHOD

Follow the instructions given for working the fire-screen, but repeat central motif twice.

1 To finish off, turn in unworked canvas edging along two long sides.

2 Cut out rectangle of backing material, adding a 2.5cm/1in seam allowance.

3 Turn under hem and tack into place.

4 Machine stitch hem on two shorter ends.

5 Place wrong sides together and slip stitch backing material into place along long edges.

6 Finish off by trimming canvas on two shorter ends.

7 Turn in and work the fringe at either end, by cutting the cotton fringing into 23cm/9in lengths.

8 Take four lengths of cotton, fold in half. Push the crochet hook through the canvas from front to back. Loop over the bunch of cotton threads and pull through.

9 Thread ends through loop thus created and pull up firmly to form a knot.

10 Continue this way until fringe is complete on both ends of the rug. Trim, if necessary, to neaten ends.

FLORENTINE-WORK FOOTSTOOL

FLORENTINE EMBROIDERY is made up of counted stitches on an even ground. It is said that this type of work was brought to Hungary by the Magyars as early as 895 AD. It has been known in Britain since the sixteenth century, when it was worked on furnishings in vibrant pinks, golds, purples and blues. Over the centuries, the examples which remain have been muted by sunshine and dust to produce lovely soft shades, which blend and tone to give wonderful effects.

The footstool worked here is in dark pink, soft pink and cream and employs the traditional and striking stitches shown in the diagram (see working instructions and chart).

MATERIALS

piece of canvas measuring 46 × 46cm/18 × 18in
Twilleys SEW tapestry wools:
4 skeins each of the following colours
68 – dark pink ◣
67 – mid pink ✕
58 – cream ╱
tapestry needle
footstool

MEASUREMENTS

The finished measurements are 32 × 38cm/12½ × 15in

The easiest way to calculate the amount of canvas required for a particular footstool is to measure the size of the old cover and add an extra 5cm/2in on each side to allow for turning. If you have no old covering as reference, measure from one side to the other lengthways and crossways, using any previous upholstery marks as a guide and allow 2.5–5cm/1–2in for padding and 5cm/2in for turning.

Florentine stitch

FIRESIDE COMFORT
This handsome and practical Florentine-work footstool tones perfectly with the muted shades of the Victorian tiles and period fireside chair

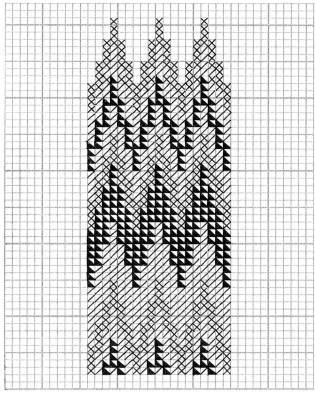

<u>METHOD</u>

1 Prepare canvas (see instructions for needlepoint fire-screen on page 48).

2 Work the canvas as shown on the chart, starting and finishing as described in previous instructions (page 48–50).

3 When the work is complete, pin out and leave to dry. Do not press.

4 To mount on footstool, make sure that the pad of wadding is sound and, if it is not, replace with suitable filling. Centre the canvas on the stool and, using flat-headed tacks secure firmly in place, stretching slightly and pulling in to shape as you work. Tuck in the corners of the canvas neatly and put in an extra tack on either side of the corner. When the canvas is applied to your satisfaction, cover the tacks with a toning braid and tack into place with round-headed upholstery tacks. Alternatively, if you do not feel up to the task, take the stool to your local craftsman, who will upholster your stool professionally.

BERLIN-WORK CUSHION AND CHAIR SEAT

B ERLIN WORK was a term generally applied to work done on canvas with wool, silk or beads. The most usually worked canvas was and is Penelope (the easiest canvas to work) or Patent or German canvas. This has the threads placed at even distances and ensures regular work.

Berlin-work embroidery was the great 'rage' of the mid-eighteen hundreds. A new method of dyeing wools was invented, producing vivid bright colours, previously undreamed of. The Victorian homemaker seized upon these colours with delight and set about cheering her household scene with a variety of items in this simple, easily worked style. Manufacturers were soon producing kits in a variety of styles and the popularity of Berlin work was to last until Edwardian times.

Some advice given to Victorian needlewomen remains sound today: always buy sufficient materials for the piece of work at one time. This is especially true of grounding colours, which may vary significantly from one dye lot to another.

MATERIALS

51 × 152cm/20 × 60in piece of Penelope canvas
tapestry frame
Twilleys SEW tapestry wools:
3 skeins each in the following colours

22 – dark pink	×
23 – medium pink	\
21 – light pink	◢
44 – dark green	+
45 – medium green	◣
46 – light green	●
37 – dark blue	■
35 – medium blue	⊻
76 – light blue	○
6 skeins of 59 – cream	/

tapestry needle
0.5m/½yd of upholstery velvet
3m/3yd matching cord
matching sewing thread
38cm/15in cushion pad
Algerian fibre
upholstery tacks

MEASUREMENTS

Finished size approx 38 × 38cm/15 × 15in

METHOD

1 For the cushion, cut one square of canvas 51 × 51cm/20 × 20in and hem and mount on frame (see page 48). Work this square in cross stitch following the chart.

2 When the square is worked, cut a square of velvet measuring 41 × 41cm/16 × 16in (or, in the case of the example in the photograph, 36 × 41cm/14 × 16in) and place right sides together with the finished tapestry.

3 Cut four lengths of cord, approx 31cm/12in and insert one on each side approx 2.5cm/1in away from each corner, levelling the end of the cord with the edge of the fabric.

4 Machine stitch around three sides close to stitching. Trim canvas and velvet at corners. Turn right side out and insert cushion pad.

5 Turn in raw edges and slip stitch firmly into place.

6 Apply cord around edge of cushion, looping at corners and slip stitching with small, neat stitches.

7 To finish off cord, tuck ends neatly together behind a corner loop. Oversew very firmly and slip stitch into position.

8 Use extra stitches to hold loops in position.

9 Finally, knot end of each of the four cord ties about 8cm/3in from cut end. Fray and unravel cord to form a tassel.

10 On the remaining square of canvas, draw the shape of the chair seat, allowing an extra 8cm/3in all round for turning in and slight padding. Work the motifs within this inner shape, making sure that the lines of colour will match up when in place on the chair.

11 Using Algerian fibre, shape the seat of the chair, to a depth of about 8cm/3in. Turn in seam allowance on finished needlepoint seat cover and, using small tacks, fix into place, leaving a small aperture for further stuffing.

12 Stuff with Algerian fibre through small hole and then finish off with tacks, pulling firmly over stuffing. Finish off with braid and upholstery tacks.

A FOCAL POINT

A Berlin-work cushion and chair seat provide a
lively accent in this quiet corner. A crocheted doily
surrounds freshly-baked buns in a circlet of frills

Cross stitch

FRAMED DORSET BUTTONS

DORSET BUTTONS were first produced in the town of Shaftesbury in the seventeenth century. They soon became popular in many parts of the world and were exported as far afield as America and Canada. A skilled worker could, apparently, produce up to 144 in a day and for this work was paid the magnificent sum of 3s 6d.

Best-quality buttons were sewn on to pink paper sheets and sent for export, second quality on blue paper and third quality on yellow were reserved for the home market.

These buttons can, today, be used on a variety of garments or one or more made in silk and tiny beads can be arranged on a velvet board to produce an interesting and decorative picture.

MATERIALS

a selection of fine wire, metal or plastic rings
scraps of fine wool, cotton embroidery thread or silk
few tiny glass or pearl beads (optional)
round-ended wool needle
embroidery needle
small amount of dark blue velvet or silk
gold or brass picture frame

METHOD

1 Tie the thread on to the ring and work a few buttonhole stitches over the ring, making sure to catch down the loose end as you work.
2 Continue to work in buttonhole stitch around the ring, pushing the stitches close together as you progress, making sure that the ring is completely covered (diagram 1).
3 When you are sure that you can fit no more stitches on to the ring, slip stitch the thread through the purl of the first buttonhole stitch to close.
4 All the stitches must now be turned to the inside, so all the purls are facing inwards and the outer surface is quite smooth. This process is called 'slicking'.

5 Keeping your thread at the top back of the ring, bring it down to the bottom and then up to the centre. Secure with your thumb and turn the ring slightly, continuing to wind the thread over and over until all the spokes of the circle are made. Be sure to space these spokes evenly as this will affect the finished look of the button.
6 Secure the spokes by making two anchoring stitches like a small cross (diagram 2). Tighten this cross firmly to make sure that the spokes stay in a central position.

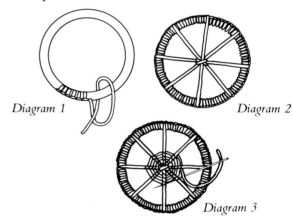

Diagram 1   Diagram 2

Diagram 3

7 The button is now filled by working a back stitch over each spoke until complete (diagram 3).
8 Change your blunt needle for an embroidery needle and finish off by making a few oversewing stitches into the back of the work.
9 Carefully run the thread to the centre of the button and leave. This thread can be used to attach the button to the backing fabric of your picture.

To include beads, work in the same manner, but thread beads on to the thread before making the spokes and place three or four beads on each spoke. When working the backstitches, make sure to space the beads evenly down each spoke.

By arranging the spokes in differing groups, a variety of effects can be achieved.

THE TEA TRAY

SUGAR BASIN AND MILK JUG COVERS

NOTHING CONJURES UP memories of Sunday tea-time at Grandma's better than these easy-to-make covers, which provide a final decorative and useful touch to the afternoon tea tray.

MATERIALS

medium-sized saucer
marker pen
sharp scissors
25cm/¼yd fine cotton net
48 medium-sized clear glass beads
15 assorted medium-sized blue glass beads
1 × 20g ball Twilleys No 20 crochet cotton
1.25 crochet hook

ABBREVIATIONS

st – stitch
sts – stitches
ch – chain
dc – double crochet [single crochet]*
sl st – slip stitch
*[USA equivalent]

MEASUREMENTS

These covers can be used on any average-sized sugar basins or milk jugs.

METHOD

1 Using a medium-sized saucer and a fabric marker pen, draw a circle on the net. Cut out with sharp scissors.
2 Thread the beads on to the crochet cotton and then work a dc through a mesh hole on the edge of the net circle. Continuing in dc, work round circle, finishing with a sl st into first dc stitch. Work a chain of 5 sts, *

miss 3 ch, dc into next st, 5 ch rep from * all round circle, sl st to first of the first 5 st ch.
3 Following the diagram, continue until row 5 has been completed. Slide first bead up to crochet hook and work into edging as shown.
4 Continue to work from the diagram until edging is completed. Sl st to first chain of last round. Finish off and sew in ends.
5 Rinse under cold running water to remove marker pen marks. Dry and press gently.
6 Repeat to make milk jug cover, increasing number of rounds of crochet and beads if necessary.

It is important that you use cotton net for these covers – nylon net is too stiff and will not hang over the basin or jug properly.

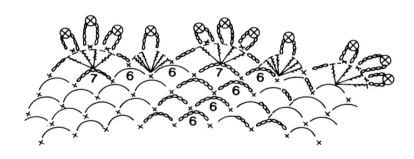

TEAPOT STAND

MATERIALS

13 metal or plastic rings 3cm/1¾in diameter
6 metal or plastic rings 2cm/¾in diameter
3 skeins of Twilleys Lystra embroidery thread in mid-blue – 95
or an odd ball of No 20 crochet cotton or 4-ply wool
wool needle
sharps sewing needle

MEASUREMENTS

The teapot stand illustrated opposite measures 17cm/6¾in

METHOD

1 Each ring must first be covered with yarn. Secure one end of the thread with a small knot on to the first ring and, using the wool needle, work all round in buttonhole stitch. Push all the stitches close together until you have completed the ring (diagram 1).

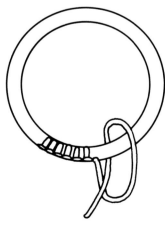

Diagram 1

2 Cut off the thread, leaving about 8cm/3in. Thread this through the needle and pass through top of first stitch to prevent a gap.

3 Pass the needle through a few stitches on the back of the ring and trim off the end.
4 Complete the remaining rings in the same way.
5 Lay the finished rings face down on to a flat surface, following the design in diagram 2.

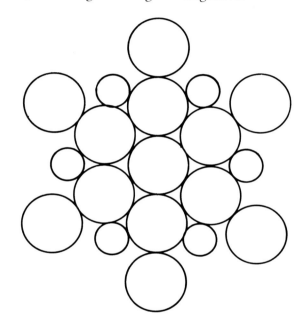

Diagram 2

6 Sew the rings together where they touch with a few small stitches, working from the centre of the design outwards until the design is complete.

The size of the mat can be altered or the design varied by adding more rings if required.

TIME FOR TEA
Embroidered teatime accessories coordinate with the Victorian blue-and-white china and an unusual but easily made teapot stand. A delicate crocheted sugar basin cover completes the set

TEA-TRAY SET

The traditional scalloped edge of this tea-tray set is taken from the shellfish of that name and refers to an edging of small semi-circles. Scallops have long been used as a decorative finish and can be worked, as here, with buttonhole stitch, or (on larger projects) faced with bias binding.

MATERIALS

(sufficient to make tray cloth, napkins and tea-cosy)
marker pen
1.5m/1½yd white cotton
medium-weight card
pair of compasses
pencils
ruler
tracing paper
scissors
dressmaker's pins
45° set square
0.5m/½yd medium-weight wadding
sewing cotton

Twilleys Lystra stranded embroidery cotton in the following colours:
2 skeins of
95 – mid-blue
45 – mid-green
3 skeins of 1 – white
1 skein of 37 – yellow
embroidery needle
sharp embroidery scissors
1m/1yd white cord

PREPARATION

1 Before starting to work, it is advisable to test the marker pen on a small piece of your fabric. Make a few marks with the pen on the edge of a scrap of fab-

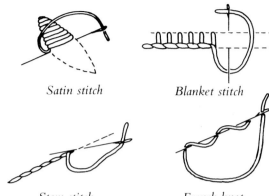

Satin stitch   Blanket stitch

Stem stitch   French knot

ric. Leave to dry and then wash out following the maker's instructions (using cold water with no detergent). Hang up to dry and examine fabric for signs of the marker. This test will avoid any unfortunate disappointments and a great deal of work, should the marking ink not wash out of your chosen fabric.

2 Make your templates: take the piece of card and, with the compasses, draw two circles: 1 × 5cm/2in diameter and 1 × 4cm/1⅝in diameter. Cut these circles out carefully and draw a line through the centre of each. Cut along these lines. (You now have four semi-circles.)

3 Before starting to cut fabric, straighten it by drawing out threads and cutting along these lines.

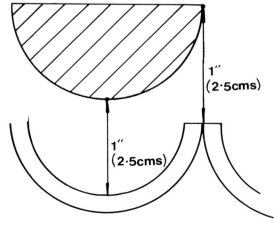

1"
(2·5cms)

1"
(2·5cms)

Diagram 2

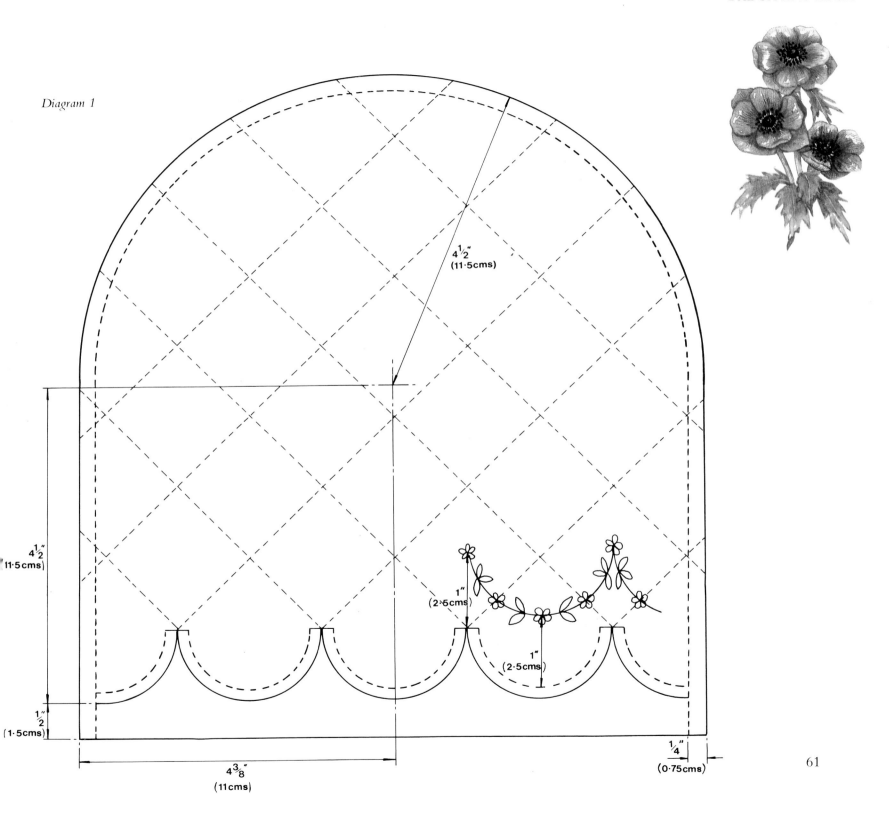

Diagram 1

4½"
(11·5cms)

4½"
(11·5cms)

1"
(2·5cms)

1"
(2·5cms)

½"
(1·5cms)

4⅜"
(11cms)

¼"
(0·75cms)

Diagram 3

TEA-TIME TEA-COSY

MEASUREMENTS

Finished measurement of cosy is 23 × 23cm/9 × 9in.

METHOD

1 Using diagram 1 (page 61), photocopy the outline of the tea-cosy using enlarging facility until tea-cosy measures approximately 220 × 240cm/9 × 9½in. Cut out and pin to the white cotton. In this way cut out 4 pieces. Then, using the same pattern, pin to wadding and cut out 2 pieces.

2 Lay 2 pieces of material on a flat surface. Using the marker pen, measure and draw a line 1.25cm/½in up from bottom edge.

3 Measure along this line to find the centre point and mark with a dot.

4 Starting from this dot, draw the scalloped design by placing the 5cm/2in diameter semi-circular template on to the material. Draw around this, repeating along the bottom edges of both pieces of material (diagram 1).

5 Now, using the smaller semi-circular template, draw another row of semi-circles on to the material, approx 0.75cm/¼in up from the previously drawn semi-circles (diagram 2).

6 Measure 2.5cm/1in up from the centre of the middle semi-circle and mark position with a dot. Measure 2.5cm/1in up from border line and mark with a dot. Using the 5cm/2in template draw another semi-circle – the dots acting as a guide (diagram 2). Draw in flowers and leaves along this line, as shown in diagram 3.

7 Using a 45° set square and ruler, draw on 45° quilting lines (diagram 1).

8 Repeat steps 5, 6 and 7 on second piece of material.

9 Place a piece of wadding on the wrong side of each of the two pieces of material and tack together.

10 Hand sew the quilting lines, using small running stitches, or machine stitch carefully. Be sure to take the stitches to the edge of the material.

11 Place both sections together, right sides facing. Tack around sides and top seam, leaving the bottom edge open. Machine around these three sides, leaving a 0.75cm/¼in seam. Turn right sides out.

12 Place remaining two pieces of white fabric together and machine a seam around edge, leaving

bottom edge open. Place inside tea-cosy to form a lining, pin and tack edge of lining and tea-cosy together at opening.

13 Start by embroidering border edge. Using two strands of white embroidery thread, blanket stitch (see diagram page 60) between the two outer semi-circular lines drawn on the cloth (diagram 3). These stitches should be placed as close together as possible.

14 When this border is complete, and using very sharp embroidery scissors, carefully trim off excess material as near to the stitches as possible, but without cutting into them.

15 Embroider flowers and leaves using satin stitch and stems using stem stitch. Complete by placing a french knot in the centre of each flower (see diagrams on page 60).

16 When complete soak in cold water to remove marker pen, wash carefully, lightly starch and press gently on wrong side.

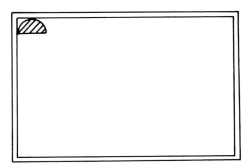

Diagram 4

Diagram 5

TRAY CLOTH AND NAPKINS

MEASUREMENTS

Finished size of tray cloth is 32 × 47cm/12½ × 18½in
Finished size of napkins is 26 × 26cm/10½ × 10½in

METHOD

1 From the remaining material cut out three pieces, one measuring 48 × 33cm/19 × 13in and two measuring 28 × 28cm/11 × 11in. These must be cut accurately.

2 Take the larger piece of material and, using the marker pen, draw a line 1.5cm/½in from cut edge on all sides (diagram 4).

3 Repeat step 2 with the two remaining pieces of fabric.

4 Place each piece of material flat and, using the 5cm/2in semi-circular template, draw in the inner and outer semi-circles as before (diagrams 2 and 5).

5 Repeat around all edges of each piece of material.

6 Following step 6 of tea-cosy instructions (page 62), draw in flowers and leaves from diagram 3 for tray cloth and diagram 6 for napkin corners.

7 Embroider border edges as described in steps 13 and 14 of tea-cosy and flowers and leaves as described in step 15.

8 Complete as for step 16 of tea-cosy.

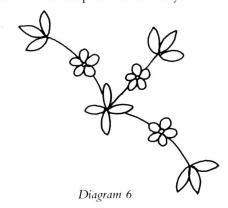

Diagram 6

63

FRILLED DOILY

MATERIALS

3 balls 20g Twilleys No 40 crochet cotton in white
1.00 crochet hook

MEASUREMENTS

25cm/10in excluding frill
43cm/17in including frill

TENSION

First 3 rounds to 5cm/2¼in

ABBREVIATIONS

ch – chain
dc – double crochet [single crochet]*
sl st – slip stitch
tr – treble [double crochet]
sp – space
lp – loop
d tr – double treble [treble]
to make a group – leaving last loop of 4 d trs [treble] on hook,
draw yarn through remaining loops on hook
*[USA equivalents]

METHOD

Commence with 14 ch, sl st into 1st ch to form a ring.
1st round: 3 ch 45 d trs into ring, sl st into top of 3 ch.
2nd round: 5 ch * miss 1 d tr, 1 d tr into next d tr, 2 ch rep from * to end, sl st into 3rd of 5 ch (24 sps).
3rd round: Sl st into sp, working into same sp as sl st work 4 ch 3 d trs, leaving last loop of each d tr on hook, draw yarn through remaining loops on hook – 1st group worked – * 3 ch, 1 group into next sp, rep from * to end, finish 3 ch, sl st into top of group.
4th round: 1 dc into sp * 6 ch, 1 dc into next sp, rep

from * to end, finish 6 ch, sl st into 1st dc.
5th round: Sl st into 2 ch, 1 dc into sp * 8 ch 1 dc into next sp rep from * to end, finish 8 ch, sl st into dc.
6th round: Sl st into sp, 4 ch, 10 d trs into same sp as sl st, 1 dc into next sp * 8 ch, 1 dc into next sp, 11 d trs into next sp, 1 dc into next sp rep from * to end, finish 8 ch, 1 dc into next sp, 1 dc into top of 4 ch.
7th round: * (3 ch miss 1 d tr, 1 dc into next d tr) 5 times, 6 ch 1 dc into next sp, 6 ch, 1 dc into 1st d tr rep from * to end, finish 6 ch, sl st into dc.
8th round: Sl st into 3 ch sp, 1 group into same sp as sl st * (2 ch, 1 group) into each of next 4 sps (8 ch 1 dc) into each of the next 2 sps, 8 ch, 1 group into 3 ch sp, rep from * to end, finish last rep, 8 ch, sl st into top of group.
9th round: Sl st into 2 ch sp, 1 group into same sp as sl st * (2 ch, 1 group) into the next 3 sps (8 ch 1 dc) into the next 3 sps, 8 ch, miss 1 group. 1 group into 2 ch sp, rep from * to end, finish 8 ch, sl st into top of group.
10th round: Sl st into 2 ch sp, 1 group into same sp as sl st * (2 ch, 1 group) into the next 2 sps (8 ch 1 dc) into the next 4 sps, 8 ch, miss 1 group. 1 group into 2 ch sp, rep from * to end, finish 8 ch, sl st into top of group.
11th round: Sl st into 2 ch sp, 1 group into same sp as sl st * 2 ch, 1 group into next sp (8 ch 1 dc) into the next 5 sps, 8 ch, miss 1 group. 1 group into next sp rep from * to end, finish 8 ch, sl st into top of group.
12th round: Sl st into 2 ch sp, 1 group into same sp * (8 ch 1 dc) into the next 6 sps, 8 ch, 1 group into 2 ch sp, rep from * to end, finish last rep 8 ch, sl st into top of group.
13th round: Sl st into 4 ch, 1 dc into sp (8 ch 1 dc) into each sp to end, finish 8 ch, sl st into dc.
14th round: Rep 13th round, working 9 ch instead of 8 ch (56 sps).
15th round: Sl st into 4 ch, 1 dc into sp * 7 ch 12 d trs into next sp (7 ch 1 dc) into next 3 sps, 7 ch 12 d trs into next sp (7 ch 1 dc) into next 2 sps, rep from * to end, finish last rep 7 ch, sl st into dc.
16th round: Sl st into 3 ch, 1 dc into sp * 6 ch, miss 6 d

trs, 1 dc between d trs (6 ch 1 dc into each sp) 4 times. 6 ch miss 6 d trs, 1 dc between d trs (6 ch, 1 dc into each sp) 3 times. Rep from * to end, finish sl st into 1st dc and into sp (72 sps).

17th round: 4 ch, 11 d trs into next sp, 12 d trs into each sp to end, sl st into top of 4 ch (864 d trs).

18th round: (3 ch 1 dc) into each d tr to end, finish 3 ch, sl st into sl st (864 sps). Place a coloured marker thread at end of round and carry through to final round.

19th round: sl st into sp (4 ch 1 dc) into each sp to end.

20th round: Sl st to centre of sp, rep to end as 19th round.

21st and 22nd rounds: Rep 20th round, with 5 ch 1 dc instead of 4 ch 1 dc.

23rd and 24th rounds: Rep last round, with 6 ch.

25th and 26th rounds: Rep last round, with 7 ch.

27th round: Rep last round with 8 ch.

28th round: Rep last round with 9 ch. Fasten off. Starch lightly and press.

SILK-COVERED BOX

MATERIALS

metal ruler
HB pencil
sheet of grey board 51 × 76.5cm/20 × 30in approx
set square
cutting board
heavy-duty craft knife (fitted with new blade)
scalpel
0.25m/¼yd grey or white felt (depending on colour of main fabric)
Copydex or similar adhesive
dressmaker's scissors
fine needlework scissors
toning sewing thread
fine curved needle
0.25m/¼yd silk, cotton or linen fabric
0.25m/¼yd contrasting silk, cotton or linen fabric
0.25m/¼yd medium-weight wadding
1m/1yd braid or ribbon trim
sheet of lightweight cardboard
fine paintbrush

MEASUREMENTS

To make a box measuring 14 × 21cm/5½ × 8¼in

METHOD

1 Using the ruler and lead pencil, draw the following rectangles on to the grey board: two rectangles measuring 20 × 10cm/8 × 4in; two rectangles measuring 14 × 10cm/5½ × 4in. Check each corner carefully to ensure that it is a right angle, using the set square, and draw each edge independently – do not use a previously cut edge to form the edge of the next rectangle.

2 Using a cutting board or a pile of newspaper to cut over, cut out the rectangles, using the heavy-duty craft knife and metal ruler. Do not use too much pressure – several shallow cuts will be more effective than one very heavy cut. Check each pair of rect-

angles to ensure that they match perfectly and that each set is of the correct height, ie 10cm/4in. (This cutting is essential to produce an accurate box.)

3 The short edges of each rectangle must now be mitred. Draw a line approx 4mm/⅛in in from each 10cm/4in edge. Hold the metal ruler along this pencil line and, using the scalpel, shave off a small amount of card to produce a sloping edge. Try not to cut away any of the previously cut edge as you work (diagram 1).

4 Lay the grey or white felt flat and place the rectangles over it, mitred edges facing upwards.

5 Lift each rectangle and paint it thinly with Copydex. Replace and press down. Leave to dry thoroughly.

6 Cut roughly around the felt and then trim closely to grey board using sharp scissors.

7 Press the covering fabric carefully to remove any creases and lay it flat, right side down. Place the rectangles, felt sides down, over the fabric as shown in diagram 2. Trim round the fabric, leaving a turning seam of 2cm/¾in on each edge.

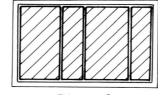

Diagram 1   *Diagram 2*

8 Paint a small amount of Copydex approx 6mm/¼in away from each edge.

9 Turn over seam allowance along each long edge, pulling the fabric slightly to reduce any puckering. Press down on to glued surface until stuck firmly.

10 Being careful to mitre the corners, turn over seam allowance on short edges and press down to secure. A small dab of glue may be necessary to secure corners, but do try to keep 6mm/¼in from corner. Leave for 20–30 minutes to dry thoroughly.

11 Using a toning sewing thread and a fine curved needle, put free edges together and invisibly slip stitch into place (diagram 3). Do keep the stitches as tiny and invisible as possible. At the end of the first row of stitches, turn and stitch back to starting point. Fasten off securely by oversewing firmly.

12 Decide which is the base of the box and carefully measure the rectangle produced by the four sides. This measurement should be absolutely accurate and be taken from inner edge to inner edge, stretching the sides outwards very slightly to ensure the finished base will sit firmly in position.

13 Draw out this rectangle on to grey board and cover with felt as before, again trimming felt closely.

14 Cover with silk fabric, leaving seam allowance and turning and sticking as in step 10.

15 Place the base into position and invisibly slip stitch firmly as before (diagram 4). Stitch all around base twice and fasten off securely.

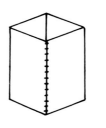

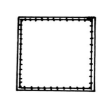

Diagram 3   *Diagram 4*

16 From the grey board cut a rectangle 15.5 × 22cm/6¼ × 8¾in to form a lid, checking the corners with the set square as before.

ON A ROMANTIC NOTE
This silk-covered box and folder add the finishing touch to a traditional writing desk placed beneath the sitting-room window

17 Paint one side of this rectangle with Copydex and cover with wadding. Trim wadding close to all edges.
18 Cover lid with silk fabric as before, mitring the corners carefully and keeping the glue away from the edges. Stretch the fabric slightly, but do check that the wadding is still smooth.
19 At this point look at the top of the lid and decide which is to be the front edge and which the back. Carefully measure the longest edge of the lid along the back edge and mark the centre point with a small dot on the inner surface.
20 Mark the centre point of the back of the box in the same way. (It is advisable to put the stitched corner to the back of the box).
21 Cut a rectangle of covering fabric, measuring approx 38 × 12cm/15 × 5in. Fold in half and machine stitch short edges together using a 1.5cm/½in seam. Press seam open, turn fabric to the right side and press flat, keeping the seam line central, (diagram 5).

Diagram 5

22 Paint sufficient Copydex on to the inner back wall of the box on either side of the centre mark to anchor the sewn rectangle of fabric.
23 Carefully matching up the seam line on the fabric with the centre point of the box wall, press the hinge

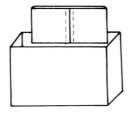

Diagram 6

flap into position (diagram 6). Leave to dry completely before continuing.
24 Matching up seam line and centre point on inside lid, paint lid with Copydex and press down remaining fabric of hinge flap. This must be done as accurately as possible, as this step will determine how the lid sits on the finished box.
25 Decide whether you will use a braid or ribbon trim and cut suitable lengths, allowing an extra 7.5cm/3in on each length. On inner surface of lid measure and mark points for glueing braid. Put the braid in position on upper surface of lid and turn under to stick down.
26 From the lightweight cardboard cut a rectangle measuring 22 × 16cm/8¾ × 6¼in. Cover one side with felt and lining fabric as before.
27 Paint the entire inner surface of the lid with Copydex, keeping the glue at least 0.75cm/¼in away from edges and apply lining board, pressing wrong sides together. Cover with a heavy book and leave to dry completely.
28 From the lightweight cardboard cut a rectangle approx 14 × 20cm/5½ × 8in. This measurement will vary from box to box, so it will be necessary for you to measure the inner dimensions of your box to determine the size of base required. Cover with felt and fabric as before.
29 Paint wrong side of inner base with Copydex and carefully push into position inside box.
30 Measure each of the four sides very accurately and cut out a rectangle to fit each side. Cover as before and glue into position.
31 Finally, turn the box around so that the back is facing you. Using a fine paintbrush paint a little extra Copydex carefully between the hinge and lid and press firmly together. This will ensure that the lid feels firm when the box is opened. However, great care must be taken to prevent glue seeping on to the outside of the box. Leave to dry thoroughly before using.

SILK-COVERED FOLDER

MATERIALS

metal ruler, pencil, set square
heavy-duty craft knife
cutting board or sheet of wood and newspapers
1 sheet of heavyweight grey board
0.5m/½yd medium-weight wadding
Copydex adhesive
0.5m/½yd × 90cm/36in felt
1m/1yd of medium-weight silk fabric 90cm/36in wide
selection of ribbons and braids for trimming
sheet of lightweight white card

MEASUREMENTS

Finished measurement approx 30.5 × 30.5cm/12 × 12in

METHOD

1 Using the ruler and pencil and checking corners with the set square, draw out the following on to the grey board; two squares 30.5 × 30.5cm/12 × 12in; one rectangle 4 × 30.5/1½ × 12in.

2 Cut out these shapes with the craft knife, using the ruler as a guide. This should be done on a cutting board or a sheet of wood, protected by several layers of newspaper.

3 Bevel one edge of each square and the two long edges of the rectangle, by placing the ruler approx 0.75cm/¼in from edge and cutting with a sloping blade along edge.

4 Lay wadding flat and paint Copydex on outer side of both squares and the rectangle. The bevelled edge should slope inwards from the outer side. Place board, glued side down, on to felt (diagram 1), with each piece as close as possible to its neighbour.

5 Leave to dry thoroughly and trim excess wadding away, close to all edges.

6 Using the felt-covered board as a template, cut out a rectangle of silk, allowing an extra 5cm/2in all round.

7 Paint Copydex approx 2.5cm/1in in from edge, around the inner side of the board. Leave for a few minutes and then turn over silk and press down over glue. Fold the two short edges first and then the two long. Mitre corners carefully as you work and be sure to pull the fabric slightly. Leave to dry.

8 Decide where the braid and ribbon trim is to go. Cut suitable lengths and put in place. Paint a small amount of glue on the ends of each piece and stick down on inner side of board.

9 Cut the following pieces from the lightweight white card: two squares 29 × 29cm/11½ × 11½in; one rectangle 2.5 × 29cm/1 × 11½in. Paint with Copydex on one side and cover with felt, see steps 4 and 5 for wadding. Use this board as a template to cut out silk fabric and cover as before (steps 6 and 7).

10 Cut a length of ribbon 40cm/15¾in and paint a small amount of glue on each end. Place the ribbon on the centre of the second board, turn ends to back and press into position. Leave to dry.

11 Cut two 23cm/9in lengths of braid and put a small amount of glue on one end of each piece. Place these glued ends 7.5cm/3in in from centre of each short side of silk- and wadding-covered board.

12 Paint a generous amount of Copydex over inner side of silk- and wadding-covered board and carefully place inner side of second board over this, making sure that the inner rectangles are centred up accurately. Do not paint glue too close to edges of silk, as this may leak out and spoil the finished effect.

13 Weight the folder down with heavy books and leave for two hours until the glue is completely dry.

14 Carefully close folder and, using braids, tie a small bow to close.

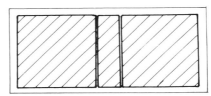

Diagram 1

CHAIRBACK AND ARMREST COVERS

DECORATIVE CHAIRBACKS developed from the antimacassars of the Victorian era – items designed to protect the furniture from the macassar hair oil used by gentlemen to pomade their hair. This manly fashion changed, but the women of the household continued to make chairbacks with matching armrest covers to embellish the sitting-room.

MATERIALS (FOR ONE SET)

10 × 20g balls of Twilleys No 20 crochet cotton in white or ecru
1.25 crochet hook
1.50 crochet hook for motif

MEASUREMENTS

Chairback – 45cm wide × 50cm long/
17½in wide × 19½in long (excluding motifs)
Armrests – 45cm wide × 29.5cm long/
17½in × 11½in (excluding motifs)

TENSION

Width – 5 sps to 2.5cm/1in
Depth – 6 rows to 2.5cm/1in

ABBREVIATIONS

ch – chain
tr – treble [double crochet]*
dc – double crochet [single crochet]
sp – space
sl st – slip stitch
rep – repeat
blk – block
in – inch/es
h tr – half treble [half double crochet]
cm – centimetres
*[USA equivalents]

1 lacet consists of: 3 ch, 1 dc into sp or miss 2 tr, 1 dc into next tr, 3 ch, 1 dc into tr or miss 2 tr, 1 tr into next tr.

1 block consists of: 1 tr into tr, 5 trs into sp, 1 tr into tr.

1 bar consists of: 5 ch, miss 5 sts, 1 tr into next st.

Always turn with 5 ch.

CHAIRBACK

METHOD

Using 1.25 crochet hook, commence with a chain of 177 sts.

1st row: 1 tr into 6th ch from hook * 2 ch, miss 1 ch, 1 tr into next ch, rep from * to end, making 86 sts.

2nd row: 14 sps, (3 ch, 1 dc into next tr, 3 ch, 1 tr into next tr) 5 times, 16 sps (3 ch, 1 dc into next tr, 3 ch, 1 tr into next tr) 3 times, 16 sps, (3 ch, 1 dc into tr, 3 ch, 1 tr into next tr) 5 times, 14 sps.

3rd row: 14 sps, (5 ch, miss 1 dc, 1 tr into next tr) 5 times, 16 sps, 3 bars, 16 sps, 5 bars, 14 sps.

4th row: 14 sps, 3 ch, 1 dc into sp, 3 ch, 1 tr into tr, 5 trs into sp, 1 tr into tr, 1 lacet, 1 blk, 1 lacet, 16 sps, 1 lacet, 1 blk, 1 lacet, 16 sps, (1 lacet, 1 blk) twice, 1 lacet, 14 sps.

5th row: 14 sps (1 bar, 1 blk over blk) twice, 1 bar, 16 sps, 1 bar, 1 blk, 1 bar, 16 sps (1 bar, 1 blk) twice, 1 bar, 14 sps.

6th row: 14 sps, 5 lacets, 16 sps, 3 lacets, 16 sps, 5 lacets, 14 sps.

7th row: 14 sps, 5 bars, 16 sps, 3 bars, 16 sps, 5 bars, 14 sps.

8th and 9th rows: rep 4th and 5th rows.

IN TRADITIONAL STYLE
Protect your upholstery with this classic set of crocheted armrests and antimacassar

10th row: 14 sps, 5 lacets, 8 sps, 11 lacets, 8 sps, 5 lacets, 14 sps.

11th row: 14 sps, 5 bars, 8 sps, 11 bars, 8 sps, 5 bars, 14 sps.

12th row: 14 sps, (1 lacet, 1 blk) twice, 1 lacet, 8 sps (1 lacet, 1 blk) 5 times, 1 lacet, 8 sps, (1 lacet, 1 blk) twice, 1 lacet, 14 sps.

13th row: 14 sps (1 bar, 1 blk) twice, 1 bar, 8 sps (1 bar, 1 blk) 5 times, 1 bar, 8 sps (1 bar, 1 blk) twice, 1 bar, 14 sps.

14th and 15th rows: rep 10th and 11th rows.

16th row: 14 sps, (1 lacet, 1 blk) twice, 1 lacet, 8 sps, 1 lacet, 1 blk, 1 lacet, (2 ch, 1 tr into centre ch, 2 ch 1 tr into next tr) 5 times, 1 lacet, 1 blk, 1 lacet, 8 sps, (1 lacet, 1 blk) twice, 1 lacet, 14 sps.

17th row: 14 sps, (1 bar, 1 blk) twice, 1 bar, 8 sps, 1 bar, 1 blk, 1 bar, 10 sps, 1 bar, 1 blk, 1 bar, 8 sps, (1 bar, 1 blk) twice, 1 bar, 14 sps.

18th row: 14 sps, 12 lacets, 10 sps, 12 lacets, 14 sps.

19th row: 14 sps, 12 bars, 10 sps, 12 bars, 14 sps.

20th row: 14 sps, (1 lacet, 1 blk) twice, 2 lacets, (1 blk, 1 lacet) 3 times, 10 sps, (1 lacet, 1 blk) 3 times, 2 lacets (1 blk, 1 lacet) twice, 14 sps.

21st row: 14 sps (1 bar, 1 blk) twice, 2 bars (1 blk, 1 bar) 3 times, 10 sps, (1 bar, 1 blk) 3 times, 2 bars (1 blk, 1 bar) twice, 14 sps.

22nd and 23rd row: rep 18th and 19th rows.

24th row: 14 sps, (1 lacet, 1 blk) twice, 1 lacet, 8 sps, 1 lacet, 1 blk, 1 lacet, 10 sps, 1 lacet, 1 blk, 1 lacet, 8 sps, (1 lacet, 1 blk) twice, 1 lacet, 14 sps.

25th row: rep 17th row.

26th–29th rows: rep 10th, 11th, 12th and 13th rows.

30th and 31st rows: rep 10th and 11th rows.

32nd–35th rows: rep 4th, 5th, 6th and 7th rows.

36th–39th rows: rep last 4 rows.

40th row: 14 sps (1 lacet, 1 blk) twice, 1 lacet, 38 sps, (1 lacet, 1 blk) twice, 1 lacet, 14 sps.

41st row: 14 sps, (1 bar, 1 blk) twice, 1 bar, 38 sps, (1 bar, 1 blk) twice, 1 bar, 14 sps.

42nd row: rep 6th row.

Rep from 3rd to end of 41st row.

Next row: 14 sps, 5 lacets, 38 sps, 5 lacets, 14 sps.

Next row: 14 sps, 5 bars, 38 sps, 5 bars, 14 sps.

Next row: 14 sps, (1 lacet, 1 blk) twice, 1 lacet, 38 sps, (1 lacet, 1 blk) twice, 1 lacet, 14 sps.

Next row: 14 sps, (1 bar, 1 blk) twice, 1 bar, 38 sps, (1 bar, 1 blk) twice, 1 bar, 14 sps.

Rep last 3 rows 4 times more.

*Next row: 14 sps, 29 lacets, 14 sps.

Next row: 14 sps, 29 bars, 14 sps.

Next row: 14 sps, (1 lacet, 1 blk) 14 times, 1 lacet, 14 sps.

Next row: 14 sps, (1 bar, 1 blk) 14 times, 1 bar, 14 sps.

Rep from * once.

Next row: 14 sps, 29 lacets, 14 sps.

Next row: 14 sps, 29 bars, 14 sps.

Next 6 rows: 86 sps.

Fasten off.

Edging

Working along side, commencing at the bottom edge, join yarn into corner ch, 5 ch, miss 1 tr, 1 dc, into next 2 sps, * 5 ch, miss 2 tr 1 dc into next 2 sps, rep from * along side across the top and along 2nd side.

2nd row: * 2 dc, 4 ch, sl st into 4th ch from hook (picot formed), 4 dc, 1 picot, 2 dc into sp, rep from * to end.

Fasten off.

Motifs

Using 1.50 crochet hook

First motif: Commence with 6 ch, sl st into 1st ch to form a ring.

1st round: 16 dc into ring, sl st into 1st dc.

2nd round: 6 ch, * miss 1 dc, 1 tr into next dc, 3 ch, rep from * 6 times, sl st into 3rd of 6 ch.

3rd round: 5 dc into each sp, sl st into 1st dc.

4th round: Sl st into next 2 dc, 9 ch, 1 tr into centre dc of next 5 dc of sp * 7 ch, 1 tr into next centre dc rep

72

from * 5 times, 7 ch sl st into 3rd of 9 ch.

5th round: 1 dc, 4 trs, 1 picot, 3 trs, 2 ch, 1 dc into bottom edge of chairback, 2 ch, 4 trs, 1 dc into same sp as last trs on motif, 1 dc, 4 trs, 2 ch, miss 3 sps on back, 1 dc into next sp, 2 ch, 3 trs, 1 picot, 4 trs, 1 dc into same sp as last trs on motif * (1 dc, 4 trs, 1 picot, 3 trs, 1 picot, 4 trs, 1 dc) into each of the next 6 sps on motif.

Fasten off.

Second motif: As 1st to end of 4th round above.

5th round: 1 dc, 4 trs, 1 picot, 3 trs into sp, 2 ch, 1 dc into centre tr between picots on 2nd scallop before joining on 1st motif, 2 ch, sl st into bottom of 1st 2 ch to form a picot on 2nd motif, 4 tr, 1 dc into same sp as last trs, 1 dc, 4 trs into next sp, 2 ch, 1 dc between picots on next scallop on 1st motif, 2 ch, sl st into bottom of 1st 2 ch, 3 trs, 1 picot, 4 trs, 1 dc into sp, 1 dc, 4 trs, 1 picot, 3 trs into next sp, 2 ch, miss 6 sps on back, 1 dc into next sp, 2 ch, sl st into bottom of first 2 ch, 4 trs, 1 dc into same sp, as last trs on motif, 1 dc, 4 trs into next sp, 2 ch, miss 3 sps on back, 1 dc into next sp, 2 ch, sl st into bottom of 2 ch, 3 trs, 1 picot, 4 trs, 1 dc into same sp as last trs. Continue to end from * on 5th round on 1st motif.

Continue in this way until 7 motifs are joined.

Finish last join at the edge of back.

ARMRESTS

Using 1.25 crochet hook, commence with a chain of 177 sts.

1st row: 1 tr into 6th ch from hook * 2 ch, miss 1 ch, 1 tr into next ch, rep from * to end (86 sps).

2nd row: 14 sps (3 ch, 1 dc into next tr, 3 ch, 1 tr into next tr) 5 times, 16 sps, (3 ch, 1 dc into next tr, 3 ch, 1 tr into next tr) 3 times, 16 sps, (3 ch, 1 dc into next tr, 3 ch, 1 tr into next tr) 5 times, 14 sps.

Continue from 3rd to end of 41st row as given for chairback.

Next row: 14 sps, 5 lacets, 38 sps, 5 lacets, 14 sps.

Next row: 14 sps, 5 bars, 38 sps, 5 bars, 14 sps.

Next row: 14 sps, (1 lacet, 1 blk) twice, 1 lacet, 38 sps, (1 lacet, 1 blk) twice, 1 lacet, 14 sps.

Next row: 14 sps, (1 bar, 1 blk) twice, 1 bar, 38 sps, (1 bar, 1 blk) twice, 1 bar, 14 sps.

Cont from * on chairback, working 14 sps each end of row until 6 rows remain.

Next 3 rows: 86 sps.

Fasten off.

Edging

As given for chairback.

Motifs

Make and join as chairback, missing 9 sps instead of 6 sps at the bottom of chairback.

CHAPTER 4
THE BEDROOM

FEMININE AND DAINTY, the cottage bedroom has all the frills and flowers associated with our idea of the perfect country room. The flower theme is reflected in the subtle fragrances of lavender sachets and sleep pillows, surely recalling a more leisured and elegant time.

The centrepiece of the bedroom – the bed – should, of course, be covered with a suitably stunning coverlet. In the past a variety of crafts has been employed for making bedcovers: knitting or crochet were popular in Victorian and Edwardian times, using a heavy cotton yarn, but the most economical and ubiquitous coverlet of all was the patchwork quilt made from scraps which were cheap and readily available. Here, we provide instructions for making a beautiful, and traditional, Durham-style quilt.

An old travelling basket can be placed at the foot of the bed to store extra bed-linen and, during the summer months, a bedroom fireplace looks wonderful filled with an arrangement of dried flowers.

Use the bedroom to display prized possessions – dolls or toy trains from your childhood, family photographs, or, even grandma's favourite nightie hanging on a coathanger!

Why not take a floral subject from your curtains or wallpaper and make a collection of china, fabrics or photographs featuring this flower, and use these objects further to adorn and personalise the room?

LAVENDER AND LACE
There is no more traditional scent for a country bedroom than lavender, captured here in a beautiful heart-shaped silk sachet

LAVENDER SACHETS

MATERIALS

tracing paper
soft lead pencil
sheet of brown paper
scissors
pins
sharps needle
matching sewing cotton
0.25m/¼yd of pale green or lavender silk or satin
0.75m/¾yd ruffled cream edging lace
scraps of cream insertion lace (or bobbin-lace corner)
cream sewing cotton
1 skein Twilleys Lystra embroidery cotton – no 2 – cream
0.25m/¼yd muslin
50g/2oz dried lavender heads
small plastic funnel
lavender essential oil (optional)
cotton wool (optional)

MEASUREMENTS

Measurement across widest point 11.5cm/4½in

METHOD

1 Using tracing paper and soft lead pencil, transfer heart shape from diagram 1 to brown paper. Cut out and use as a pattern piece to cut two hearts from silk or satin.

2 Pin edging lace to right side of one heart shape, having edges together, and following curves by gathering lace slightly as you work. When the shape is completed, hand seam the two raw edges of lace together neatly, oversewing with tiny stitches to finish. The lace join is better placed at the point of the heart, mitring the join slightly to ensure that the lace lies correctly. Tack lace into position around heart shape.

3 Take second heart shape and tack insertion lace into position, folding and tacking a corner if necessary. When satisfied with the effect, machine stitch into position.

4 Draw monogram initial (diagram 2) in a central position and embroider with cream thread, using satin stitch and french knots (see diagram).

5 Place right sides of hearts together, tack and sew, leaving a small opening for inserting lavender sachet. Remove tacking stitches, snip seam curves to allow for easing and trim away excess fabric at point. Turn to right side and press lightly.

6 Using the heart pattern, cut out two muslin shapes, slightly smaller than the silk or satin hearts. Sew together, again leaving a small opening. Turn inside out and fill with lavender. This is easily done by pouring the lavender flowers through a small plastic funnel inserted into the opening. Turn in a narrow seam and slip stitch opening firmly together.

7 Carefully insert the lavender sachet into the case, turn in seam and slip stitch together with toning cotton.

Note Before closing the muslin lavender sachet, a small piece of cotton wool impregnated with a few drops of lavender oil can be added with the flower heads. Be careful not to use too much, however, as the oil may stain the silk or satin covering.

Diagram 1

Satin stitch   *French knots*

Diagram 2

A B C D E

F G H I J

J K L M

N O P Q R

P T U V

W X Y Z

SCENTED COATHANGER

RIBBONWORK HAS BEEN popular since the nineteenth century, when manufacturers produced a wide range of shaded and plain ribbons in a vast selection of colours and widths. Nowadays, it is impossible to recreate the delicate work of the Victorians, but many uses can be found for the ribbon roses and leaves used to adorn this pretty coathanger.

MATERIALS

1 wooden coathanger
0.5m/½yd of pale green silk or satin
dressmaker's pins
soft lead pencil
scissors
0.5m/½yd of medium-weight wadding
25g/1oz of dried lavender flowers
few drops of oil of lavender
sharps needle
matching sewing cotton
a tube of Superglue
bodkin
a length of pale mauve embroidery silk or cotton
0.25m/¼yd of Offray 7cm single-faced satin ribbon in the following colours:
413 – pale lavender
430 – light orchid
463 – grape
510 – ice mint
513 – pastel green
530 – mint

METHOD

1 Unscrew hook from coathanger. Fold silk material in half and pin together. Using the wooden coathanger as a template, draw out a curved rectangle on to the silk with the lead pencil. Draw a seam line 1.25cm/½in out from this line. Cut out approx 1.25cm/½in again from this second line.

2 Lay the coathanger on the wadding and cut out a rectangle which is slightly wider than the coathanger, measured end to end, and approx six times as wide, measured top to bottom.

3 Put the lavender heads into a small bowl and sprinkle with a few drops of essential oil. Leave until the oil is absorbed before continuing.

4 Sprinkle the lavender heads on to the wadding and wrap carefully but loosely around the coathanger. Secure in position with a few running stitches at each end and along top edge.

5 Put the two right sides of the silk or satin material together and machine along bottom edge and both ends. Fold in half from short end to short end and mark centre with a pencil. Now machine one top edge from outer edge to within 0.75cm/¼in of pencil mark.

6 Trim seams and cut across corners to within a fraction of the sewing line. Turn right side out and press. Turn in raw edges to the depth of seam and press under.

7 Carefully push one end of the coathanger into the cover. Push the other end into the opposite corner, bring up cover and slip stitch top seam into position, leaving a tiny gap in the middle to allow the hook to be replaced.

8 Using a small spot of Superglue, attach one end of the embroidery silk to the outer end of the hook, laying the thread along the metal so that the loose end is at its tip. Leave to dry and then carefully wrap the thread around the hook, pushing each strand close to the next until the hook is covered as far as the screw. When this point is reached, put a little Superglue on

THE SCENTS OF SUMMER
Filled with lavender and decorated with delicate ribbonwork roses in pastel shades, this delightful scented coathanger is the perfect addition to a country bedroom

the hook and bind over carefully with thread, making sure not to touch the hook with the fingers. Leave to dry thoroughly.

9 Using a bodkin, make a hole in the wadding over the hole in the coathanger and, putting a little glue on the tip, screw the hook back into position.

10 Using the satin ribbon, make a selection of roses and leaves (see below).

11 When you have made sufficient roses and leaves in a variety of colours, sew them firmly to the coathanger around the base of the hook, making sure to tuck the rough ends well out of sight to produce a close bunch of flowers.

RIBBON ROSES

1 Thread a needle with thread to match your ribbon and knot the end.

2 Roll one end of the ribbon into a tight tube, turning about three times.

3 Oversew one end of the tube (diagram 1). This forms the heart of the rose.

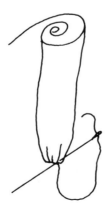

Diagram 1

4 Drop the needle and let the thread hang while you fold the ribbon diagonally outwards (diagram 2).

5 Bring round fold to form a petal and stitch in place.

6 Turn the rose around and repeat steps 2 and 3 until

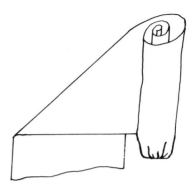

Diagram 2

the required number of petals has been made. Sew firmly at the base.

7 To finish off: loop the ribbon down to base and cut off squarely. Gather and stitch in position.

RIBBON LEAVES

1 Using green ribbon, satin side outwards, fold and cut as shown in diagram 3.

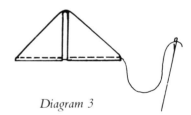

Diagram 3

2 With matching green thread, knotted at one end, gather by running a row of tiny straight stitches through all thicknesses of ribbon.

3 Pull thread up fairly loosely. Finish by oversewing firmly.

MONOGRAMMED LINEN

THE USE OF INITIALS and numbers has always been important in the art of embroidery. Indeed lettering as part of an overall design has been used since the Middle Ages, particularly featuring in German whitework. The Victorians expanded on this tradition and many pattern books were published, often employing Gothic or Old English lettering. Interest in this craft declined somewhat after the two World Wars, but gradually, with the return of white table and bed-linen, monograms are again becoming fashionable.

MATERIALS

tracing paper
2B lead pencil
2 white cotton or linen pillowcases either handmade or purchased
(see instructions on page 83)
1 white cotton/linen sheet (optional)
1 skein of Twilleys Lystra embroidery thread in the following
colours:
52 – pale green
69 – pale pink
97 – grey
53 – mid-green
1 – white
sharps needle
1m/1yd 4in of lace 10cm/4in wide (to trim each pillowcase) either
purchased or see instructions on page 84

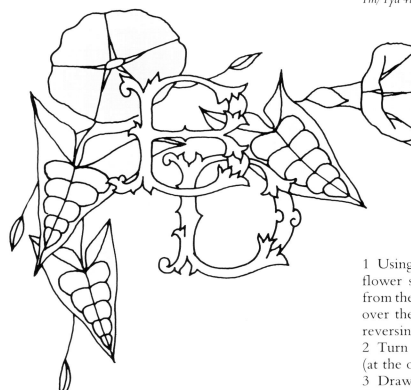

METHOD

1 Using the tracing paper and pencil, trace off the flower spray, replacing the initials with your own from the alphabet on pages 82–3. Turn over and draw over the pencil lines again on the wrong side, thus reversing the design.
2 Turn over again and lay over corner of pillowcase (at the open end).
3 Draw over the pencil lines again, transferring your design to the pillowcase ready for embroidery.
4 Repeat with second pillowcase, but make sure that

81

the design is on the opposite corner so that each monogram will be on the outer edges of the bed. You will need to reverse the letters within the design to achieve this.

5 Repeat this procedure on the outer edges of a matching sheet if required.

6 Now, using satin stitch, embroider the initials in grey. Leaves and stems should be worked in green, using satin and stem stitches (see diagrams). The bindweed flowers should be worked in pink satin stitch, with highlights picked out in white.

7 When the work is completed, wash to remove pencil marks, lightly starch and press.

Satin stitch   *Stem stitch*

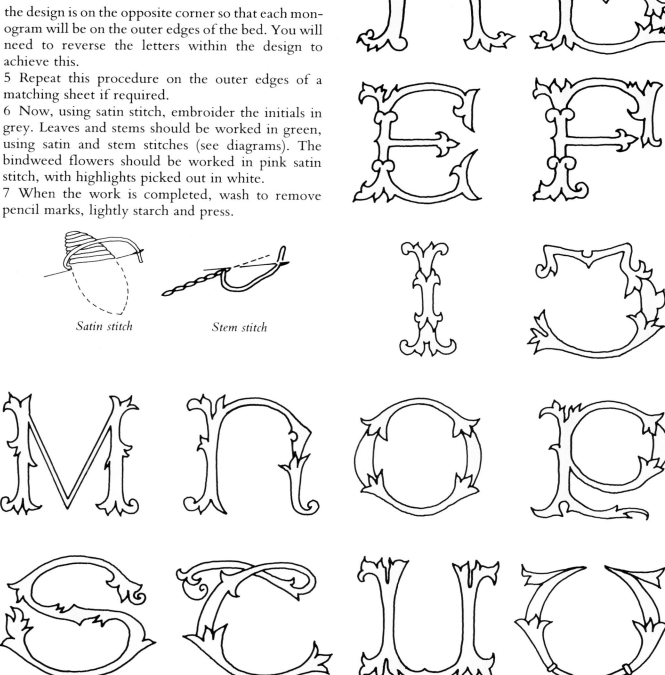

PILLOWCASES

MATERIALS

1m/1yd good-quality white cotton/linen 90cm/36in wide
scissors
cotton sewing thread
dressmaker's pins
tacking cotton

MEASUREMENTS

Finished size of pillowcase 76 × 46cm/30 × 19in approx

METHOD

1 To straighten fabric, draw out warp and weft threads close to edges and cut along these lines.
2 Now cut two rectangles, one 78 × 48cm/31 × 19in and a smaller rectangle 48 × 22.5cm/19 × 9in.
3 Turn in a 1.25cm/½in hem along one long edge of the smaller rectangle and hand sew or machine in place. Press firmly.
4 Taking one of the two larger rectangles, pin unhemmed longer edge of small rectangle to a short side, right sides together and machine stitch with a 1.25cm/½in seam.
5 Fold over and press. Tack into place along side-seam lines, using long running stitches.
6 Turn a 1.25cm/½in hem on one shorter side of second rectangle and hand sew neatly into place. Press.
7 Put right sides of two larger rectangles together, baste in place, leaving the hemmed edges open and machine a 1.25cm/½in seam along other three sides.
8 Turn pillowcase right side out and decorate with monograms.

CROCHET EDGING FOR PILLOWCASE

MATERIALS

1 × 20g ball of Twilleys Forty in white
0.75 crochet hook

MEASUREMENTS

depth: 7½cm/3in
length: 1m/1yd 4in

ABBREVIATIONS

ch – chain
tr – treble [double crochet]*
dc – double crochet [single crochet]
sp – space
*[USA equivalents]

METHOD

Make 23 ch.
1st row: 1 dc into 7th ch from hook, 3 ch, miss 2 ch, (1 tr into next ch, 1 ch, miss next ch) 3 times, 1 tr into next 8 ch.
2nd row: 6 ch, miss 3 tr, 1 tr into next 4 tr, (1 ch, 1 tr into next tr) 3 times, miss next ch sp, 8 tr into next ch sp.
3rd row: 3 ch (1 tr between next 2 tr) 7 times, 1 tr into next 2 tr, (1 ch, 1 tr into next tr) 3 times, 1 tr into next 3 tr, 3 tr into ch sp, 1 tr into 3rd of 6 ch.
4th row: 6 ch, miss 3 tr, 1 tr into next 4 tr, (1 ch, 1 tr into next tr) 3 times, (1 ch, 1 tr between next 2 tr) 9 times, 1 ch, 1 tr into top of 3 ch.
5th row: 4 ch, (1 tr between next 2 tr, 1 ch) 10 times, 1 ch, 1 tr into next tr (1 ch, 1 tr into next tr) 3 times, 1 tr into next 3 tr, 3 tr into ch sp, 1 tr into 3rd of 6 ch.
6th row: 6 ch, miss 3 tr, 1 tr into next 4 tr (1 ch, 1 tr into next tr) 3 times, (1 ch, 1 tr between next 2 tr) 11 times, 1 ch, 1 tr into 3rd of 4 ch.

7th row: 4 ch (1 tr between next 2 tr) 12 times, 1 ch, 1 tr into next tr, (1 ch, 1 tr into next tr) 3 times, 1 tr into next 3 tr, 3 tr into ch sp, 1 tr into 3rd of 6 ch.
8th row: 6 ch, miss 3 tr, 1 tr into next 4 tr (1 ch, 1 tr into next tr) 3 times, (1 ch, 1 tr between next 2 tr) 13 times, 1 ch, 1 tr into 3rd of 4 ch.
9th row: 4 ch (1 tr between 2 tr) 14 times, 1 ch, 1 tr into next tr, (1 ch, 1 tr into next tr) 3 times, 1 tr into next 3 tr, 3 tr into ch sp, 1 tr into 3rd of 6 ch.
10th row: 6 ch, miss 3 tr, 1 tr into next 4 tr, (1 ch, 1 tr into next tr) 3 times, (5 ch, miss next ch sp, 1 dc into next ch sp) 7 times, 5 ch, work (1 dc, 5 ch, 1 dc) into last ch sp.
Now work down side of fan thus: 5 ch, 1 dc into end of next row, (5 ch, miss next row, 1 dc into end of next row, 5 ch, 1 dc into end of next row) twice, 5 ch, 1 dc into same space as 8 tr, turn.
11th row: (5 ch, 1 dc into next ch sp) 6 times, 5 ch (1 dc, 5 ch, 1 dc) into next ch sp, (5 ch, 1 dc into next ch sp) 8 times, 5 ch (1 tr into next tr, 1 ch) 3 times, 1 tr into next 4 tr, 3 tr into ch sp, 1 tr into 3rd of 6 ch.
12th row: 6 ch, miss 3 tr, 1 tr into next 4 tr (1 ch, 1 tr into next tr) 3 times, (5 ch, 1 dc into next ch sp) 9 times, 5 ch (1 dc, 5 ch, 1 dc) into next ch sp, (5 ch, 1 dc into next ch sp) 7 times, 5 ch, 1 dc into same space as 8 tr, *turn.*
13th row: (5 ch, 1 dc into ch sp) 8 times, 5 ch (1 dc, 5 ch, 1 dc) into next ch sp (1 ch, 1 dc into next ch sp) 10 times, 5 ch (1 tr into next tr, 1 ch) 3 times, 1 tr into next 4 tr, 3 tr into ch sp, 1 tr into 3rd of 6 ch.
Repeat 2nd to 13th rows for pattern. Continue in pattern until length required, ending with a 13th row. Fasten off.
Sew in ends. Press lightly and slip stitch into position on open end of pillowcase.

TABLECLOTH TRIMMED WITH KNITTED LACE

MATERIALS

8 × 20g balls Twilleys Twenty in white or ecru
1 set 2½mm/no 13 knitting needles
2m/2yds of 90cm/36in wide fine linen or heavy cotton fabric
sewing thread
sharps needle
dressmaker's pins

MEASUREMENTS

Finished measurement of cloth is
137 × 137cm/54 × 54in approx

ABBREVIATIONS

st – stitch
sts – stitches
k – knit
p – purl
yrn – yarn round needle
sl st – slip stitch
psso – pass slip stitch over
m1 – make a stitch by knitting twice into next stitch

EDGING

Using no 13 needles, cast on 29 sts and k 1 row. Then work in pattern as follows:
1st row: (right side): K2, k2 tog, yrn, k7, yrn, sl 1, k2 tog, psso, yrn, k2, k2 tog, yrn, sl 1, k1, psso, k3, yrn, sl 1, k2 tog, psso, yrn, k2 tog, k1 (27sts).
2nd row: Yrn, k2 tog, k7, k1, p1 into yrn of previous row, knit to last 6 sts, k2 tog, yrn, k4 (28 sts).
3rd row: K2, k2 tog, yrn, k5, k2 tog, yrn, k3, yrn sl 1, k1 psso, k5, k2 tog, yrn k3, yrn, k2 (29 sts).
4th row and all even rows unless otherwise stated: Yrn, k2 tog, k across to last 6 sts, k2 tog, yrn k4.
5th row: K2, k2 tog, yrn, k4, k2 tog, yrn, k5, yrn sl 1, k1, psso, k3, k2 tog, yrn, k5, yrn, k2 (30 sts).

7th row: K2, k2 tog, yrn, k3, k2 tog, yrn, k7, yrn sl 1, k1, psso, k1, k2 tog, yrn, k7, yrn, k2 (31 sts).
9th row: (K2, k2 tog, yrn) 3 times, sl 1, k1, psso, k3, yrn sl 1, k2 tog, psso, yrn, k2, k2 tog, yrn, sl 1, k1, psso, k3, yrn, k2 (30 sts).
10th row: Yrn, k2 tog, k5, k1 and p1 in to the next yrn of previous row, k10, k1 and p1 into next yrn of previous row, k5, k2 tog, yrn, k4 (32 sts).
11th row: K2, k2 tog, yrn, k4, yrn, sl 1, k1, psso, k5, k2 tog, yrn, k3, yrn, sl 1, k1, psso, k5, k2 tog, yrn, k2 tog, k1 (31 sts).
13th row: K2, k2 tog, yrn (k5, yrn, sl 1, k1, psso, k3, k2 tog, yrn) twice, k2 tog, k1 (30 sts).
15th row: K2, k2 tog, yrn, k6, yrn, sl 1, k1, psso, k1, k2 tog, yrn, k7, yrn, sl 1, k1, psso, k1, k2 tog, yrn, k2 tog, k1 (29 sts).
16th row: As row 4.
Repeat rows 1–16 until the work measures the circumference of the cloth, plus 51cm/20in to allow 13cm/5in easing around each corner (in this case approx 530cm/212in). Cast off loosely.

85

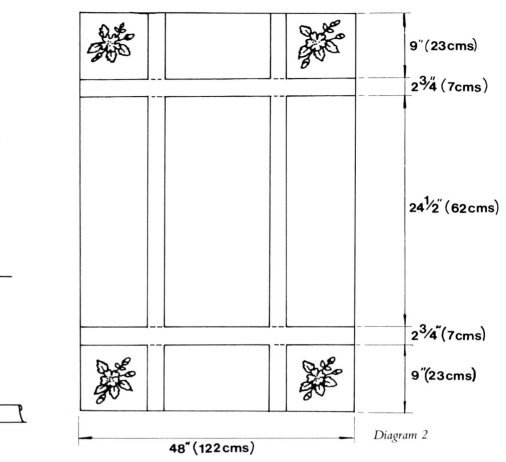

Diagram 1

9" (23cms)

2¾" (7cms)

24½" (62cms)

2¾" (7cms)

9" (23cms)

48" (122cms)

Diagram 2

KNITTED LACE INSERTION

METHOD

Cast on 25 sts.

1st row: K2, k2 tog, yrn, k7, yrn, sl 1, k2 tog, psso, yrn, k5, yrn, k4.

2nd row and all even rows unless otherwise stated: K2, k2 tog, yrn, k15, k2 tog, yrn, k4.

3rd row: K2, k2 tog, yrn, k5, k2 tog, yrn, k3, yrn, sl 1, k1, psso, k3, k2 tog, yrn, k4.

5th row: K2, k2 tog, yrn, k4, k2 tog, yrn, k5, yrn, sl 1, k1, psso, k2, k2 tog, yrn, k4.

7th row: K2, k2 tog, yrn, k3, k2 tog, yrn, k7, yrn, sl 1, k1, psso, k1, k2 tog, yrn, k4.

9th row: (K2, k2 tog, yrn) 3 times, sl 1, k1, psso, k3, yrn, sl 1, k1, psso, k2 tog, yrn, k4 (24 sts).

10th row: K2, k2 tog, yrn, k8, k and p into next yrn, k5, k2 tog, yrn, k4 (25 sts).

11th row: K2, k2 tog, yrn, k4, yrn, sl 1, k1, psso, k5, k2 tog, yrn, k2, k2 tog, yrn, k4.

13th row: K2, k2 tog, yrn, k5, yrn, sl 1, k1, psso, k3, k2 tog, yrn, k3, k2 tog, yrn, k4.

15th row: K2, k2 tog, yrn, k6, yrn, sl 1, k1, psso, k1, (k2 tog, yrn, k4) twice.

16th row: Rep row 2.

Rep rows 1 to 16 for pattern repeats. Work in pattern for the required length for each insertion, ending with row 2 of pattern.

Cast off. Block strips to required measurements.

In the above manner make the following insertion strips: 4 strips 23cm/9in long; 2 strips 122cm/48in long; 2 strips 61cm/24½in long.

TO MAKE UP TABLECLOTH

1 True fabric as described on page 83 and cut out the following: 4 pieces 26 × 26cm/10 × 10in; 4 pieces 26 × 64cm/10 × 25½in; 1 piece 64 × 64cm/25½ × 25½in. These must be hemmed with a fine hem 0.75cm/¼in and the corners mitred (diagram 1).
2 Assemble the cloth as shown in diagram 2 and slip stitch knitted insertions into place.
3 Wash edging and pin out to dry, pulling each point out and pinning firmly. When completely dry, sew commencing and cast-off edges together and pin the edging around the edge of the cloth. Ease and gather 13cm/5in around each corner. Slip stitch into place.
4 Finish the cloth by embroidering whitework sprays (see below) in positions marked in diagram 2.

WHITEWORK EMBROIDERED SPRAYS

Any white embroidery on a white background is classed as whitework, but the term is especially used to denote very fine work on sheer muslin. The most exquisite examples of whitework are the Ayrshire christening robes made during the last century. The term whitework can also be applied to any form of plain sewing and so is an appropriate term to apply to this beautiful tablecloth.

MATERIALS

tracing paper
HB pencil
embroiderer's carbon paper
2 skeins Twilleys Lystra white embroidery silk
embroidery needle
small, round embroidery frame

METHOD

1 Following the instructions on page 81, transfer a bouquet of flowers to each corner of the cloth.
2 Embroider, using 1 strand of embroidery thread, following stitch suggestions given in the diagrams.
3 Finish off neatly and press lightly on wrong side.
4 Wash and lightly starch the cloth and press gently on wrong side, pulling knitted lace into shape, or pin out on a fabric-covered board and leave to dry. Always remember to use stainless steel pins, otherwise the fabric may become marked during this process.

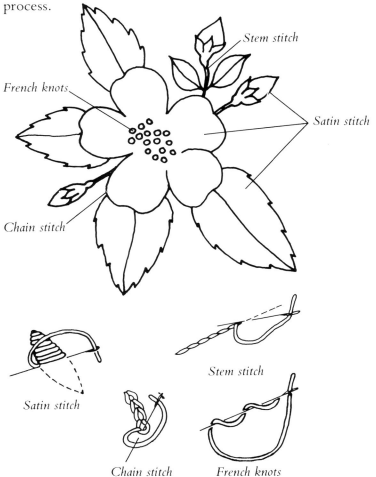

Stem stitch

French knots

Satin stitch

Chain stitch

Satin stitch

Stem stitch

Chain stitch

French knots

BEDSIDE RUG

a variety of pastel-coloured fabrics
scissors
stiff cardboard
sewing threads
sharps needles
tapestry needle
strong waxed cotton thread
non-slip backing material

MEASUREMENTS

Finished measurements approx 72 × 82cm/28½ × 32½in

METHOD

1 First cut the fabric into long strips about 5–7.5cm/ 2–3in wide. Make each strip as long as possible.
2 Fold each strip so that the raw edges meet in the middle of the fabric (diagram 1) and then bring the folded edges together and press flat (diagram 2). Wind each completed strip around a sheet of cardboard to keep it in place.

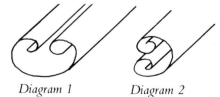

Diagram 1   *Diagram 2*

3 Start to plait by unfolding the raw edges of two strips. Sew the edges together with a bias seam (diagram 3). Trim excess fabric from corner. Refold with the raw edges inside.

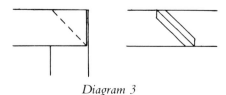

Diagram 3

4 Attach a third strip with a few running stitches to form a letter 'T' shape (diagram 4).
5 Begin plaiting by bringing the left-hand strip over the centre strip and then the right-hand strip over that (diagram 5).

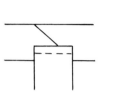 

Diagram 4   *Diagram 5*

6 Continue in this way until you finish a strip, always making sure that the folded edges are towards the centre of the plait.
7 Join in a new strip with a bias seam as before.

Note: It is advisable to work with strips of differing lengths, so that all the joins do not occur at once.

8 When you have plaited about 91.5cm/3ft begin to sew together. The easiest way to do this is by lacing (diagram 6). Thread a blunt tapestry needle with

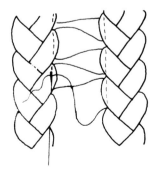

Diagram 6

strong waxed cotton thread. Draw this through the loop of one plait, then thread through the corresponding loop of the opposite plait. To make a circu-

BEDSIDE WARMTH

*This striking bedside rug in autumn colours
complements perfectly the warm tones of a
natural wood floor*

lar rug keep winding the plait round and round, but make sure that it always lies flat. Try to ease the fullness around the curves as you work.

9 As the rug nears completion, begin to reduce the size of each strip. This will make the plait narrower, enabling it to blend with the last completed row. Weave the remaining ends into the outer ring of work with a crochet hook and firmly slip stitch into position.

10 The rug can be backed with a non-slip backing material. Place the finished rug flat on the backing material and cut to shape, allowing a hem of 1.5–2cm/½–¾in. Turn in this hem and slip stitch to back of the rug.

A HOP-FILLED SLEEP PILLOW

"Rest in Aphrodite's lovely flowers"

HOPS HAVE ALWAYS been associated with sound sleep and restfulness and a little herb pillow filled with dried wild hops (and Aphrodite's lovely flower – the rose) can help to promote a peaceful night and also be a decorative addition to the bedside table. At night the sachet should be slipped into the pillowcase, so that the essence of the hops and roses can be inhaled throughout the night.

The design for this pillow has been charted in simple cross stitch in a selection of soft colours.

MATERIALS

0.25m/¼yd cream evenweave fabric
Twilleys Lystra embroidery thread:
1 skein each of the following colours

39 – buttermilk	×
41 – light green	■
45 – medium leaf green	◀
46 – light leaf green	△
51 – light olive green	▲
52 – light sage green	+
53 – dark olive green	□
65 – fuchsia pink	◣
66 – dusky rose pink	○
67 – dark pink	/
68 – medium pink	●
69 – light pink	\
52 – light sage green (backstitch)	—

0.25m/¼yd silk in pale green or pink
0.25m/¼yd fine muslin or calico
handful of dried wild hops
handful of dried scented red rose petals
toning sewing thread
sharps needle

MEASUREMENTS

Finished size is 13.75 × 18.75cm/5½ × 7½in

METHOD

Before beginning to work, find and mark the central point in the fabric. Hem and mount on frame.

1 Following chart on pages 92–3, embroider the design using cross stitches throughout (see diagram on page 93).

2 When completed cut out to a rectangle measuring 20 × 15cm/8 × 6in.

3 Cut a rectangle from the silk material, also measuring 20 × 15cm/8 × 6in.

4 With right sides together sew the embroidered fabric and the silk together, leaving one short side open for filling. Trim corners and turn right side out. Press.

5 Cut out two rectangles measuring 18 × 13cm/7 × 5in from the gauze or calico and sew up on three sides. Fill with a mixture of dried wild hops and rose petals. Hops can be gathered from the hedgerows in early autumn and hung in the kitchen to dry. When papery, remove hop heads and use to fill pillow. Do make sure, however, that they are completely dry before using. They should rustle when flicked with the finger nail. Alternatively, hops can be purchased from a home-brewing supply shop.

6 Sew up the fourth side of the pillow firmly and put inside embroidered pillowcase. Turn in a 1.25cm/½in seam on raw edges and oversew neatly.

A PERFECT NIGHT'S SLEEP

This little embroidered herb pillow, filled with dried wild hops and roses, will ensure a peaceful night for the most restless sleeper. During the day, display it with other small cushions and delicate lacework for a pretty, feminine feel

Back stitch

Cross stitch

93

DURHAM-STYLE QUILT

WADDED QUILTING, also known as Durham quilting, is arguably the most beautiful form of quilting produced in the British Isles. It consists of a top sheet of plain fabric with an interlining of sheep's wool, old blankets or, nowadays, wadding. These layers are held together by a series of close-running stitches, worked in a variety of traditional patterns. The effect of light on these patterns gives the quilt its beauty, so they are traditionally worked in white or pastel colours. However, dark-coloured chintz fabrics could also be used with very much the same effect.

MATERIALS

7m/7¾yd of white cotton fabric 190cm/72in wide
tapestry frame
7m/7¾yd medium-weight wadding 190cm/72in wide
7m/7¾yd of gauze 190cm/72in wide
tacking thread
sharps needle
large piece medium-weight card
pair of compasses
large 45° set square
metal ruler
scalpel
2 water-soluble marker pens
approx 4 large reels of white sewing cotton or quilting thread
betweens needles or sewing machine
double white sheet

MEASUREMENTS

Finished size of quilt – 241 × 191cm/95 × 75in

This quilt can be worked by hand on a frame or, with care, using a sewing machine. Obviously the traditional quilt was worked by hand – often by groups of women. The original quilting frames would have been very large and would have accommodated a whole quilt. Today it is more practical to work the

quilt in small panels. These panels are quite quick to work and are a less daunting prospect, as they can be stored away until the project is completed.

A rectangular embroidery frame made up of two long bars and two stretchers is ideal for working these panels.

TO SET UP THE FRAME

(in order to work the quilt by hand)

1 Begin by marking the centre point on each side of the fabric and the centre point on both tapes. These points should be matched up when the fabric is attached to the frame.

2 Dismantle the frame and oversew the top edge of the gauze to the tape on one rail and the bottom edge to the other.

3 Reassemble the frame and push in the pegs, making sure that the fabric is held firmly, but not too taut.

4 Lay the wadding on to the gauze. The surplus will hang over the back of the frame.

5 Place the cotton fabric over this, with the marked design uppermost. Tack along one side through all three thicknesses.

6 Smooth the top sheet of fabric over the wadding and fasten along the other side with a row of long pins. Tack into position carefully, being sure to keep all layers flat.

7 The work must now be secured at either side, so tie one end of the tape around a stretcher close to the rail.

8 Fix the tape to one corner of the work with a long needle.

9 Take the tape back around the stretcher and secure again with a needle. Continue with this all down each side at intervals of about 8cm/3in and tie off the tape at each lower corner.

Diagram 1

TO BEGIN SEWING BY HAND

1 If working with the frame on your lap, it is convenient to rest its upper edge against the back of a dining-chair.

2 To sew each section: sit comfortably at the frame and begin to work from the nearest side, from right to left.

3 Knot the thread and bring the needle from the back to the front of the work to the point where you will begin to sew. A sharp pull will bring the knot through the gauze into the wadding.

4 Work each line with a series of small, even running stitches. To enable the work to progress more quickly make several stitches before pulling the needle through.

5 Whilst working, hold your left hand under the work to help guide the needle.

6 Curves should be worked with smaller stitches.

7 Finish by making a backstitch into the previous stitch and run the remaining thread through the wadding.

95

METHOD OF WORKING AND ASSEMBLING THE QUILT

Note: The instructions below have been given for machine sewing your quilt, but it is obviously possible to substitute hand sewing, following the above instructions for setting up and working. The cutting out, pattern drawing and assembly will, of course, be the same in both methods. In the case of machine sewing, a frame will obviously not be appropriate, so great care must be taken to keep all layers of fabric flat, otherwise wrinkling will occur.

1 Using example shapes shown in diagram 1 on page 95, trace off and transfer to medium-weight card to make a selection of templates. Cut out, using a metal ruler and scalpel.

2 Draw threads in cotton fabric to true up material. This will make the finished quilt much more easily assembled.

3 Start by cutting out the fabric wadding and gauze to the sizes given below:

1 piece 102 × 76cm/40 × 30in
2 pieces 8 × 87cm/3 × 34in
2 pieces 8 × 102cm/3 × 40in
4 pieces 5 × 108cm/2 × 42½in
2 pieces 5 × 228cm/2 × 90in
2 pieces 38 × 16.5cm/15 × 6½in
24 pieces 38 × 38cm/15 × 15in
16 pieces 38 × 5cm/15 × 2in

4 Starting with the middle panel (102 × 76cm/40 ×

A FAMILY HEIRLOOM

Surprisingly simple to create, this stunning Durham-style quilt makes a superb centrepiece for the country bedroom – and one which will be treasured for generations to come

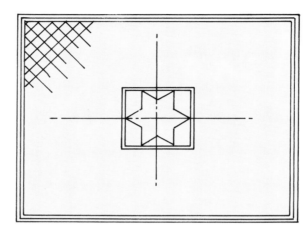

Diagram 2

Diagram 3

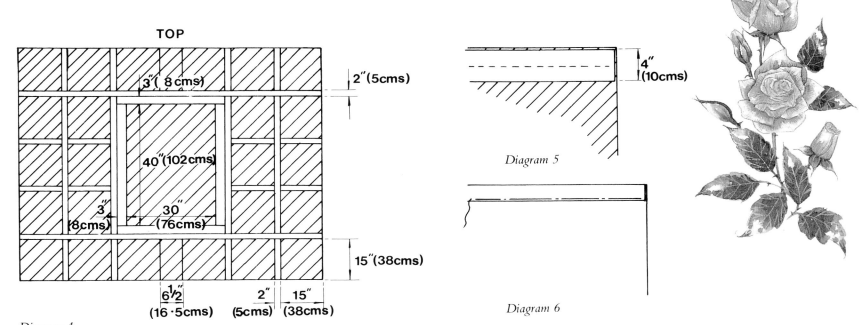

TOP

3″ (8 cms)

2″(5cms)

40″(102 cms)

3″ (8cms)

30″ (76cms)

15″(38cms)

6½″ (16·5cms)

2″ (5cms)

15″ (38cms)

Diagram 4

4″ (10cms)

Diagram 5

Diagram 6

30in), fold in half lengthways and crossways and press to find centre point. Beginning at this point, and using templates, start to draw in the pattern with a marker pen (diagram 2).

5 Sandwich top sheet of fabric together with wadding and gauze; tack around edges and across fabric from corner to corner to form a cross.

6 Repeat this procedure with the twenty-four 38cm/15in square pieces and the two 38 × 16.5cm/15 × 6½in pieces, using the design examples shown in diagram 3.

7 Hand sew (using small running stitches) or machine stitch your design on each panel, through the three layers of fabric.

8 Make sure to take all cotton ends through to wrong side.

9 The remaining strips (two 5 × 228cm/2 × 90in, sixteen 5 × 38cm/2 × 15in, four 5 × 108cm/2 × 42½in, two 8 × 102cm/3 × 40in, two 8 × 87cm/3 × 34in), although not quilted, must be tacked together to form a sandwich of fabric, wadding and gauze, in the same manner before the quilt can be assembled.

10 Now start to assemble quilt following diagram 4.

11 Machine seam, using a 1.25cm/½in seam and trim off excess material if necessary.

12 Lay the quilt flat and tack backing sheet to the wrong side of the quilt, cutting off excess material.

13 Using the remaining material cut four long strips, the length and width of the quilt, 10cm/4in wide. (It may be necessary to sew lengths of fabric together at this stage, in order to gain the necessary length). Fold in half and iron. With right sides facing, machine the edging strip to the quilt along one edge (diagram 5).

14 Do the same to the opposite side of the quilt. Fold down the edging strip and tack down to underside of quilt (diagram 6) turning in 0.75cm/¼in of fabric to form a hem.

15 Machine two remaining edging strips to quilt, fold down in the same way, making sure that the corners are neat.

16 Hem stitch all round quilt carefully.

17 Soak quilt in cold water to remove marker pen, then gently wash.

The quilt can be made smaller or larger by altering the arrangement and number of panels.

NIGHTDRESS CASE

0.5m/½yd of plain green cotton fabric 90cm/36in wide
1 sheet of dark blue dressmaker's carbon paper
HB and B lead pencils
tracing paper
cork board and drawing pins
45° set square
ruler
ready-cut mount card with an oval window measuring
11¼ × 9cm/4½ × 3½in (to use as template)
1 skein each Twilleys Lystra embroidery thread
43, 44, 46 – greens
2 – cream
39 – buttermilk
3 – coffee
4 – medium coffee
97 – light grey
0.5m/½yd lightweight wadding
0.5m/½yd pale green satin lining fabric 110cm/44in wide
matching pale green sewing cotton
cream ruffled lace (optional)
small round glass button or bead, either clear or green

MEASUREMENTS

The finished size is 33.75 × 27.5cm/13½ × 11in

METHOD

1 From green cotton cut a rectangle measuring 110 × 40cm/44 × 16in.

2 Using the tracing paper and a lead pencil, trace off the spray of honeysuckle from the pattern opposite.

3 Lay a sheet of embroiderer's carbon paper face down over the right side of the green fabric approx 25cm/10in in from one short edge.

4 Place the traced pattern over this, making sure that the bouquet is in the centre of the fabric and the centre of the flowers lies approx 30cm/12in from the short edge.

5 Carefully pin the layers together on to a cork board using drawing pins, making sure that the pattern cannot move, and draw over the design again with a hard pencil and heavy pressure, making sure that the bouquet transfers clearly.

6 Remove tracing and carbon paper and centre mount over the fabric, so that the flowers lie centrally within the oval. Using this mount as a template, draw an oval around flower design using a soft lead pencil.

7 Draw around an oval meat plate or large picture frame to round off the corners of the fabric to form a flap on the completed nightdress case as shown in the photograph or alternatively leave square. Cut around curve if necessary.

8 Draw in the quilting lines using the set square and ruler, leaving the centre of the oval unquilted.

9 Embroider the honeysuckle spray in stem stitch, satin stitch and french knots (see diagrams on page 101), using one strand of embroidery thread and referring to the pattern for colour guidelines.

10 Cut a rectangle of wadding measuring 75 × 40cm/30 × 16in and pin it into position on wrong side of green fabric. One short edge of wadding should be lined up with the curved or rectangular edge of the flap. Tack carefully to prevent wadding slipping and, if necessary run a few lines of tacking stitches across the width of the fabric to secure.

11 Using toning green thread either machine stitch or quilt along quilting lines, taking loose ends through to back of work at the end of each row.

12 If required, tack ruffled lace into position around curved or rectangular edge of upper flap, placing edges together and easing lace around curve.

13 Using green fabric as a guide, cut out lining from green satin material.

14 Place right sides together with quilted material and tack together, leaving straight short edge open for turning. Machine stitch and turn, clipping curves if necessary. Press carefully on satin side, turning in seam allowance on open edge.

15 Slip stitch opening closed using toning thread.
16 Fold nightdress case as shown in the diagram and machine stitch sides together.
17 Turn right side out.
18 Make a buttonhole loop on centre of upper flap using green embroidery silk. Fold down flap and mark centre of buttonhole loop with a light pencil mark. Sew on button and fasten off.

AND SO TO BED . . .
A charming nightdress case in delicate greens and creams rests against the soft folds of our beautiful Durham-style quilt

Satin stitch

Stem stitch

French knots

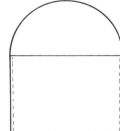

Folding the nightdress case

101

CHAPTER 5
THE BATHROOM

THE COLOURS OF SAND, shells and sky have been used to create the accessories for this room, conjuring up a feeling of holidays by the sea-shore and providing a chance to unwind in a cosy and inviting setting.

The bathroom is, obviously, a fairly modern and welcome addition to the cottage-dweller's life. It is a room, therefore, where imagination can be left to run riot, using and adapting ideas for an individual touch.

In pre-Victorian times the sanitary arrangements consisted of a chamber pot under the bed and a jug and bowl on the washstand in the corner of the bedroom. However, by the late 1880s domestic plumbing had developed into facilities occupying a whole room and would have included most of the fixtures and amenities we enjoy today.

To furnish your bathroom with a truly Victorian feeling, choose a ceramic floor covering. If space permits, a bentwood chair and towel rail are very attractive and a series of old prints or postcards will add a further decorative effect. The Victorians were particularly fond of botanical prints and these can be displayed to advantage in the modern bathroom.

A box covered with shells is particularly suitable for this room and this shell theme can be echoed in the frieze. A large shell filled with tiny shell-shaped guest soaps can further emphasise the seaside atmosphere.

THE COUNTRY BATHROOM
A deep blue painted bath enhances the warm wood shades of our unusual decorated lavatory seat, which rests on an easily-made bath mat in a natural tone.

PAINTED WOODEN LAVATORY SEAT

M ANY OLD BATHROOMS are lucky enough to have the original wooden lavatory seats still in place. If not, a new pine seat can be given a touch of character by painting with an art nouveau design.

Use your ingenuity to decorate the seat in your bathroom. The more daring artist could incorporate a few lines from some cheeky Victorian doggerel verse or the simple invitation to meditate alone for a while!

MATERIALS

1 wooden lavatory seat, stripped and sanded*
tracing paper
2B lead pencil
1 tube of blue acrylic paint
1 tube of olive-green acrylic paint
2.5cm/1in household paintbrush
medium paintbrush
1 small tin of clear varnish

* a plastic seat could be used, in which case use enamel paints and do not varnish.

METHOD

1 Following diagrams, trace designs on to tracing paper with 2B pencil.
2 Transfer design to lavatory seat by turning over, placing in position (right side down) and drawing over the lines again.
3 Each time you have used the design, you will need to go over the lines on the right side again, as the design will only transfer once.
4 Now paint in the design.
5 Leave to dry for 48 hours.
6 Cover with a thin coat of clear varnish.
7 Repeat step 6 twice more, leaving at least 12 hours between each coat.
8 For obvious reasons, it is wise to leave for 48 hours until completely dry, before using!

STENCIL FOR FRIEZE

I F YOU WISH to stencil a matching frieze around the bath or on the walls, it is possible to enlarge the art nouveau design given for the lavatory seat, by using a photocopier with an enlargement facility. Photocopy the design from the book and then keep photocopying the photocopy until you have the desired size. This motif can then be traced on to linseed-oiled stencil card, cut out with a sharp craft knife and used in the usual way.

EMBROIDERED MOTIFS
FOR CURTAINS

TRY TAKING A MOTIF from wallpaper, china, etc, to repeat on the border of embroidered curtains for a very special effect.

The motif shown on page 107 has taken the design from around the lavatory seat and this design could be repeated on a frieze around the bath or stencilled on the back of the bathroom door. Using a little imagination, any room can be personalised like this and the idea can be adapted in a variety of ways to suit the scope of the decorator.

MATERIALS

2.5m/2¾yd of cotton lawn
hard and soft lead pencils
piece of card
compasses
sharps needle
tracing paper
scissors
ruler
set square
Twilleys Lystra embroidery threads:
2 skeins each of
96 – dark blue
94 – light blue
52 – medium green
3 – beige
5 – light brown
white sewing cotton
2.5m/2¾yd of heavy white cotton lace
36 small brass rings
piece of dowelling measuring 117cm/46in

MEASUREMENTS

To fit a window measuring 107 × 107cm/42 × 42in

METHOD

1 Divide the cotton lawn in half lengthways and cut carefully, drawing a thread if necessary to true the fabric before starting to cut.
2 Lay each piece of fabric flat and, using a set square, draw a line 1.25cm/½in down from the top edge of each curtain (diagram 1).

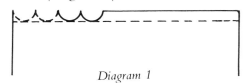

Diagram 1

3 Using the compasses, draw a circle with a radius of 3.75cm/1½in on the card. Cut out carefully. Bisect this circle and cut in half to give two semi-circles. Use one of these semi-circles to draw an inverted scalloped edge along the line at the top of each curtain (diagram 1).
4 Using sharp scissors, cut carefully along this line.
5 Turn in a tiny hem and neatly hem stitch all along this scalloped edge (diagram 2).

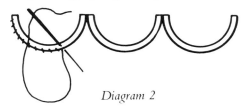

Diagram 2

6 Turn in a rolled edge along each side of each curtain and slip stitch, using tiny stitches.
7 Measure 7.5cm/3in up from the bottom edge of each curtain and draw a light pencil mark across each, using the set square.
8 Trace off art nouveau motif given for toilet seat, using tracing paper and soft pencil. Transfer pattern to curtains, along drawn line as shown in diagram 3.
9 Using stem stitch, satin stitch and french knots (see

105

Diagram 3

CROCHET EDGING FOR GUEST TOWELS

MATERIALS

1 × 50g ball of Twilleys Stalite in white
1.50 crochet hook

ABBREVIATIONS

sts – stitches
tr – treble [double crochet]*
ch – chain
lp – loop
* [USA equivalent]

METHOD

diagrams), embroider design, keeping the back of the work as tidy as possible.

10 When the embroidery is completed, turn up a narrow hem on each curtain (making sure that both measure the same). Slip stitch lace into position along bottom edges.

11 At the top point of each scallop firmly sew a small brass ring. Thread these through the dowelling and hang curtains.

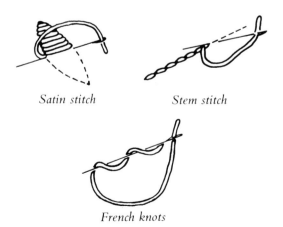

Satin stitch   *Stem stitch*

French knots

Make a chain of 16 sts.

1st row: Work 1 tr into 4th ch from hook, 1 tr into next 8 ch, 1 ch, miss 1 ch, 1 tr into next ch, 1 ch, miss 1 ch, 1 tr into last ch, turn with 4 ch.

2nd row: Miss 1st tr, 1 tr into next tr, 1 ch, miss 1 ch, 1 tr in next 6 trs, 3 ch, miss 3 ch, 1 tr into turning chain, turn with 9 ch.

3rd row: 3 tr into 3 ch lp, 3 ch, miss 3 tr, 1 tr into next 3 trs, 1 ch, miss 1 ch, 1 tr into next tr, 1 ch, 1 tr into 2nd st of turning ch, turn with 4 ch.

4th row: Miss 1st tr, 1 tr into next tr, 1 ch, miss 1 tr, 1 tr into next 3 trs, 3 trs into 3 ch lp, 3 ch, miss 2 tr, 1 tr into last tr, turn with 3 ch.

5th row: 3 trs into 3 ch lp, 1 tr into next 6 trs, 1 ch, miss 1 ch, 1 tr into next tr, 1 ch, 1 tr into 2nd st of turning ch, turn with 4 ch.

Repeat rows 2–5 until work measures 46cm/18in, or width of towel. Fasten off and sew in ends.

Make a second edging strip and slip stitch firmly to each end of the towel, making sure to fasten off securely.

FRESH AND CLEAN
A pure white guest towel is delicately embellished with crochet edging, while work continues on an embroidered art nouveau motif for bathroom curtains

BATH MAT

MATERIALS

2 hanks Twilleys dishcloth cotton
1 pair 6mm no 6 knitting needles
good quality hand towel in cream or colour to match bathroom
strong sewing thread

MEASUREMENTS

71 × 92cm/28 × 36in

TENSION

approx 3½ sts to 2.5cm/1in

ABBREVIATIONS

st – stitch
sts – stitches
k – knit
kw – knit wise
p – purl
g st – garter stitch
rep – repeat

METHOD

Cast on 101 sts.
1st row: K.
2nd row: K1, * insert right-hand needle kw into next st, wind cotton kw around this needle and first two fingers of the left hand twice, then k st passing 2 sts on to right-hand needle. Pass these 2 sts back onto the left-hand needle and k together, making one k st, k1, rep from * to end.
3rd row: P. K next 6 rows in g st.
Rep from 2nd row until the mat measures 86.5cm/34in, ending with a 3rd row. Cast off.
Back with a good quality hand towel, stitching across width of rug at each end and at several places along its length.

ROSEBUD CIRCLE

MATERIALS

7.5cm/3in Styrofoam circle (for dried flower arranging)
2 large dried red rosebuds
14 small dried red rosebuds
quantity of tiny dried flower heads (in this case very tiny pink rosebuds)
28 unopened dried rosebuds
few sprigs of dried lavender
28cm/11in of edging lace 2.5cm/1in wide
Copydex adhesive
long steel dressmaking pins

METHOD

1 Cut off the rosebud heads, leaving sufficient stalk to push into the foam circle.
2 Start by pushing the small red rosebuds into the central flattened portion of the foam circle, placing each snugly next to its neighbour.
3 Push the tiny pink rosebud heads into the inner section of the foam circle, covering it completely, but leaving two spaces in which to place the large red rosebuds.
4 Any spaces can be filled with tiny spikes of lavender.
5 The outer section should be covered with the unopened rosebuds.
6 Carefully paint Copydex on the outer edge of the foam, section by section, and gather and place the lace edging around this edge. Use the pins to hold the lace in position while the glue dries. Continue until the circle is completed.
7 The rosebud circle can be hung on the wall, by simply pressing the foam against a nail until it is secure, or placed on a small table with a chunky candle in its middle.

SHELLWORK BOX

WE ARE EXTREMELY fortunate to have a wide variety of shells available on our own seashores. Trips abroad can also be very fruitful – most of us have the odd shell or two lurking at the bottom of a drawer or box, a souvenir of some half-forgotten holiday in the sun.

The Victorians had a passion for utilising everything in a decorative and sometimes useful way. Shellwork can either be very good or extremely bad and, in order to produce a good example, a little time and consideration has to be given to the project which is to be attempted. Good shellwork is almost invariably composed of a great number of shells of the same type, grouped together in areas governed by size and colour. These shells must be placed so that they lie as close to each other as possible – large gaps must be avoided at all costs. If gaps do occur, try to fill them with the tiny microshells which can be found amongst the sand on good 'shell' beaches.

Another rule to observe when working with shells is only to use perfect, undamaged specimens – many good projects have been ruined by the haphazard use of broken shells.

It is a matter of personal taste whether or not you varnish the finished shell design. In its favour, varnishing does protect the surface from dust, and darkens and heightens the colours of the shells. However, if you prefer the soft, delicate colours which result in leaving the shells in their natural state, any dust which will inevitably collect on the box can be removed with a goose feather, or similar flight feather from a fairly large bird.

Shells can be found on most beaches. Try searching the high- and low-water lines on any beach and you will be surprised at the quantity and variety of specimens you will find. Rock pools will also yield a good supply of shells, but please take only empty shells – do not destroy their original owners in your passion for collecting.

If you are unable to collect your own shells from the seashore, do remember that shells can be gathered on river banks, lake shores and in gravel pits. And land-snail shells can also be found under hedges, on the downs and in the crevices of old walls and rock formations. Your local fishmonger may let you have shells or you can always purchase them from specialist craft shops, such as Eaton's Shell Shop, 30 Neal Street, London WC2.

MATERIALS

wooden box
newspaper
clear glue such as Araldite
selection of shells
tweezers
small tin of clear gloss varnish
2.5cm/1in paintbrush

METHOD

1 Remove hinges from the box before you start, if this is at all possible.
2 Always work with the pieces flat on a work surface, protected with newspapers.
3 A simple arrangement of small shells of uniform size is the most effective. If you intend to cover the entire box at one time, apply a thin layer of adhesive to a small area of each surface and work over that, before applying glue to the next section. Apply very small shells for additional decoration using tweezers.
4 When the entire box is covered to your satisfaction leave to dry for at least 24 hours before varnishing.
5 Using a small household paintbrush, apply a very thin coat of varnish to the entire box and leave to dry for a further 24 hours. Repeat step 5 at least twice for a good finish.
6 Refix the hinges, being careful not to dislodge any shells as you work.

SAND PICTURE

IN ORDER TO ENHANCE further the image of seaside holidays created in this cottage bathroom, why not produce a sand picture of your favourite holiday spot? These pictures were very popular in Victorian and Edwardian times and are now enjoying a well-deserved revival. Alternatively, try adapting an art nouveau or art deco design to reproduce in sand.

MATERIALS

photograph of a favourite view
approx 20cm × 25.5cm/8 × 10in
cork board or tile
drawing-pins
tracing paper
hard and soft lead pencils
piece of manilla board approx 20.5 × 25.5cm/8 × 10in
selection of coloured sands*
or
silver sand coloured with a variety of coloured inks or soot
dry gum arabic powder**
selection of tiny plastic funnels
tea-strainer
drinking straw
several wing or tail feathers from birds such as geese or ducks
steam iron
can of clear, matt spray varnish
piece of dark brown mount board 25.5 × 30.5cm/10 × 12in with
window measuring 18 × 23cm/7 × 9in
gold pen
gold ink and calligraphy pen or rub-down dry gold lettering
ruler
dark wood frame measuring 25.5 × 30.5cm/10 × 12in

* Coloured sand is available by mail order from The Needles Pleasure Park, Alum Bay, Totland, Isle of Wight, PO39 0JD. Alternatively, silver sand from any garden centre can be mixed with a small amount of a variety of coloured inks and left to dry. A traditional method of obtaining depth of colour was to mix sand with a small amount of soot. This darkened sand can be used to give definition and areas of shade, but should only be used in moderation.

** Gum arabic adhesive can be obtained by mail order from G. Baldwin & Co, Medical Herbalists, 173 Walworth Road, London SE17 1RW. It is as well to ask for gum arabic powder, otherwise the gum will have to be ground in a coffee mill!

METHOD

1 Having chosen the view you wish to reproduce, pin the photograph to a cork board with drawing-pins and lay the tracing paper over it. Secure the tracing paper with more pins and start to trace the main features, ie hills, coastline, trees, etc, using the softest lead pencil.
2 When you are satisfied with the composition of your picture, remove the pins, tracing paper and photograph.
3 Turn the tracing paper over and draw over design again. Turn over and lay it over the manilla card, making sure that the design is in the right position. Pin the edges of the tracing paper down with the drawing-pins, being careful not to pin through the card. Using a hard lead pencil, go carefully over all the drawn lines, transferring them to the card.
4 Remove pins and tracing paper and check that the design has traced off properly. Carefully go over the outline again with a soft pencil, filling in any gaps.
5 Choose the coloured sands to make up the picture, aiming to get as much contrast as possible between adjacent areas. Try out small patches of each to make sure that you will be happy with the finished result.
6 When you have chosen all the sand colours, mix three teaspoons of each with one teaspoon of powdered gum arabic in separate dishes, making sure that the adhesive is thoroughly blended.
7 Choose the area on which you will start and, using a small amount of sand and a flight feather, draw the outline of this area. Now tip a small amount of sand through the funnels or tea-strainer on to the working

area. Again using the flight feather, gently add features and textures.

8 At this point you can 'set' your picture using steam from the steam iron, or can continue to work until the whole picture is finished. It is perhaps better to set the whole picture at one go, as this allows for minor alterations as the work progresses. However, working with sand that has not been set does have the disadvantage that a small bump will upset the whole effect.

9 To produce the effect of sky, add a thin coating of sand and blow very gently through the drinking straw to produce 'clouds'.

10 When the whole picture is finished to your satisfaction, pass the steam iron over once again to ensure

SAND AND SEA

Memories of seaside holidays are recaptured in this attractive shellwork box and unusual sand picture. A charming rosebud and lace circle completes the composition

that the whole area is thoroughly set. Leave to settle for a few hours before spraying with varnish. Leave for a further 30 minutes and spray again. The picture is now finished, but should be left for 24 hours before final assembly.

11 Using the gold pen, draw a line around the edge of the window in the mount card and, if required, add the title of the view using the gold pen or gold rub-down dry lettering.

12 Put into the frame and admire the finished effect!

111

SCRAP SCREEN – DÉCOUPAGE

A SCRAP SCREEN is usually composed of three or four flat panels, hinged together. This can be used, as the Victorians would have done, to shield a favourite chair from draughts, to create an area of privacy or simply as a highly decorative wall panel.

It is possible to buy packs of reproduction scraps, but it is far more interesting and, of course, less expensive, to create your own effect by using pictures cut from magazines, old greetings cards, wrapping paper, photographs. In fact, anything to add colour and a personal touch to your project. Look in junk shops for old prints, greetings cards, even badly damaged books. These can be a useful source of supply, although it is as well to check, before cutting up something which might be potentially valuable!

Try to ensure that all your scraps are of roughly the same thickness. It is possible to use the occasional thicker piece, but too many will produce a very uneven texture, which will not varnish satisfactorily. Try to vary the colour of your scraps. Dark backgrounds look the most effective, with overlays of Victorian- and Edwardian-style cut-outs.

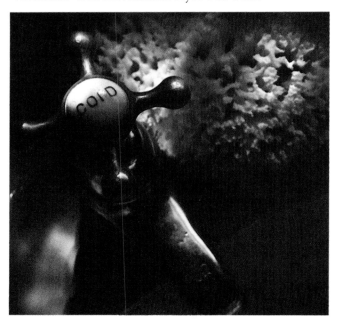

MATERIALS

(if using an old screen)

1 old, sound, panelled screen
coarse and fine sandpaper
lining material
wood to paper glue
calico
tacks 1.25cm/½in
braid
upholstery tacks
hammer

PREPARATION

1 If you are lucky enough to have an old screen as your base, remove any tacks and also the fabric covering. Check the frame for woodworm and treat if necessary. Remove hinges and rub down frame with coarse and then fine sandpaper to remove any dirt and residue.

2 Measure the height and width of each panel. If the top edge of the panel is curved, allowance will have to be made for this in the cutting. Remember to measure to the full height of the curve. Add 5cm/2in all around and, using these measurements as your guide, cut out two rectangles of calico for each panel.

3 Now using a panel as a template, cut out two rectangles of paper per panel and carefully glue these into position, one on each side of screen.

4 The calico must now be stretched across each panel and secured with small tacks down each side and across the top and bottom. Be sure to keep the grain of the fabric running true across the width and the length of each panel and stretch fairly tightly. Trim off any surplus material.

DÉCOUPAGE
A colourful scrap screen adds a lively and authentic touch to the country bathroom

5 Now following instructions on page 115 decorate screen and reassemble as given in instructions.

TO CONSTRUCT A SCREEN

MATERIALS

6 or 8 sheets of hardboard
cut to the finished size of each panel
3 wooden battens for each panel
(2.5 × 5cm/1 × 2in × width of panel)
3 wooden battens for each panel
(2.5 × 5cm/1 × 2in × length of panel)
small saw
strong wood adhesive
2cm/¾in panel pins
hammer
chisel
screwdriver
4 or 6 screen hinges and screws (two per panel)
wallpaper paste

METHOD

1 Fix three shorter-length battens across the back of three or four panels (depending on number required for finished screen). Glue into position.

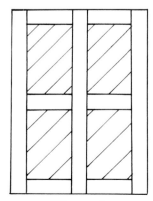

Diagram 1

2 When dry, fix three longer lengths lengthways down the back of these panels (diagram 1).
3 Leave to dry and then nail into position. Always leave the panels flat to dry and keep away from direct heat, such as a radiator.
4 Glue remaining panels into position over the battens to form a panel. If necessary, use nails around edge to secure the whole firmly.
5 Chisel out two small rectangles to enable hinges to be fitted on each panel. Fix hinges on to one panel only (diagram 2). It is easier to work on single panels, so do not assemble the screen until the *découpage* is completed.

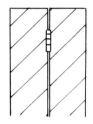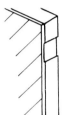

Diagram 2

6 Before starting to apply pictures, size each side of the screen with wallpaper paste (see maker's instructions on sizing) and leave to dry thoroughly.

TO DECORATE SCREEN

MATERIALS

large selection of cuttings, prints, photos, etc
adhesive (for paper to fabric use Copydex, for paper to wood
try Bostik 3)
heavy-duty brush such as a stencilling brush
chalk or a pencil
scissors
rabbit skin size
0.5l/1pt of Rowney paper varnish
2.5cm/1in paint brush
fine sandpaper (optional)
soft clean duster
4 or 6 small metal castors

You will probably find that you need far more cuttings, etc, than expected, so try to work one panel at a time.

METHOD

1 Lie each panel flat on the floor or a large table and move the prints around until you are satisfied with the results. Try putting large pieces, such as flower gardens, interior views, etc, down as a background and arrange smaller pieces over them. When you are happy with your results, glue into position.

2 If you wish, mark the position of each piece on the board, numbering as you go, and chalk the number on back of each picture. This will help in reassembling the work, if for some reason you are interrupted.

3 Start from the bottom and work upwards, smoothing out any air bubbles as you go and also wiping away any excess glue.

4 Work right to the edge of the screen.

5 Leave the panels to dry completely before varnishing. The making of a scrap screen can be a continuing project: scraps can be added for weeks or even months as suitable material comes to hand.

6 Make up the rabbit skin size according to the maker's instructions, leave until thick and then apply two coats to each side of each panel. Leave to dry thoroughly (approx 24 hours).

7 Keeping the panels flat, use long even strokes to apply the varnish as thinly as possible. Work quickly, but try not to let the varnish strokes overlap. At the end of each application, check sides for runs and remove with a brush. If the varnish run has hardened, it will have to be removed using sandpaper, but this must be done very carefully. Alternatively, spray with satin matt varnish following maker's instructions. This varnish will dry much more quickly, but many more coats will be required to give an even finish and the end result will not be as satisfactory.

8 Leave to dry thoroughly before applying another coat and make sure to dust the surface carefully. If using ordinary varnish, apply three to four coats in this way. Now check the finish of your screen. The more coats of varnish that are applied, the better the finished screen will wear. As many as twenty coats can be applied for a superb finish. Victorian screens were often sealed with shellac which will give the characteristic 'yellowed' effect to even a modern screen. Leave to dry for a week before assembling the screen.

9 Assemble the screen, by fixing the hinges as shown (diagram 2).

10 Apply small castors along lower edge to help move the screen – one at the end of each end panel and two on each end of centre panel or panels.

Découpage can be used to decorate any number of items around the house. It can look especially charming on an old suitcase, which can then be used to store table-linen, sheets, etc.

FABRIC-COVERED HAT BOX

A RANGE OF DECORATED round boxes, similar to the hat boxes of Edwardian days, can be made to complement any room in the house. In our country cottage we have used them in the bathroom to store items such as cotton wool, hair rollers and brushes or even loo rolls!

MATERIALS

pair of compasses
sheet of corrugated cardboard
35.5 × 63.5cm/14 × 25in approx
craft scissors
0.5m/½yd of 115cm/45in cotton fabric
soft pencils
metal ruler
1.3m/1⅜yd Bondaweb (bonding webbing)
1 piece of medium-weight wadding 23 × 43cm/9 × 17in
0.5m/½yd of 115cm/45in cotton lining fabric
sheet of mount board
set square
craft knife
Copydex adhesive
clothes pegs or large paper clips
braids, ribbons, flowers, etc (optional)

MEASUREMENTS

Finished measurements are diameter 61cm/24in, height 15cm/6in approx

METHOD

1 Using the compasses, draw two circles on the corrugated cardboard – 1 × 18.25cm/7¼in (box base) and 1 × 20cm/8in (box lid). Cut out carefully using craft scissors.
2 Take the larger circle (the lid) and place it on the wrong side of the cotton fabric. Carefully draw around this circle approx 5cm/1in away from the edge, to allow for a hem. Cut out along this line.

3 Now lay this fabric on the paper side of the Bondaweb and draw around the circle using a soft pencil. Cut out carefully.
4 Put the fabric, right side down, on to an ironing board and lay the Bondaweb over it, paper side up. Iron firmly with a warm iron until the Bondaweb has fused with the fabric. Peel off paper backing.
5 Use the corrugated cardboard lid to cut two circles from the wadding and make a layered sandwich thus – cardboard, two layers of wadding, fabric (Bondaweb side down). Turn this over so that the cardboard lid is uppermost and make sure that the whole lies centrally on the fabric cover.
6 Carefully cut around the edge of the fabric cover and turn in flaps. Fuse with warm iron as you work. Continue until the fabric cover is completely secured. Turn over and iron carefully over lid to fuse (diagram 1).

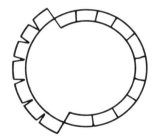

Diagram 1

7 Using this lid as a template, cut another piece of Bondaweb to this size and also a circle from the lining fabric.
8 Fuse the Bondaweb to the wrong side of the lining material as before. Peel off backing paper and centre the lining over the inner side of the lid section. Fuse. Trim edges if necessary.
9 From the mount board cut a rectangle 3.75 × 67cm/1½in × 26½in making sure (by using the set square) that the corners are right angles. Lay this rectangle over the cotton fabric and cut another rectangle, this time measuring 15 × 72.25cm/6 × 28½in. Cut out a piece of Bondaweb to this size.

10 Using the method previously described, fuse the Bondaweb to wrong side of fabric.

11 Check which way this cardboard rectangle bends most easily and put the outer side down centrally over wrong side of cotton fabric.

12 Turn in surplus fabric along top and bottom edges and fuse. Turn in end hems and fuse (diagram 2). A small piece of Bondaweb can be used to anchor down the folds if required.

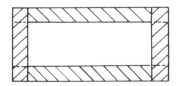

Diagram 2

13 Paint a small amount of Copydex to upper inner side of this rectangle (side lid) and carefully attach this side lid to lid by bending and shaping side lid to fit firmly around lid edge. Keep pressing firmly until

A FLORAL WINDOW

A useful fabric-covered hat box echoes the delicate cotton print and flower-patterned net of the curtains, to create a charming floral windowsill display

glue dries. This step forms box lid.

14 There will be a small amount of overlap on the side lid. This must be glued together firmly using Copydex. Be sure not to paint the glue too close to the edges, to prevent any leaking. Hold together with paper clips or clothes pegs until completely dry.

15 Using the smaller circle make the box base as box lid, omitting the layers of wadding (see steps 2–8).

16 Cut a rectangle 13.75 × 68.75cm/5½ × 27½in to form the side wall of the box and assemble as for side lid.

17 Attach base to side wall as before and leave to dry thoroughly.

18 The hat box can now be trimmed with a variety of braids, ribbons, flowers, etc, as required.

CHAPTER 6
THE GARDEN

FOR CENTURIES THE country garden has been a retreat from the cares of the world. The cottage garden of our dreams is perfect in every detail, from the rustic arches and trellis-work over which perfumed roses climb, to the medieval sundial, gently marking the steady passage of time.

The country garden is marked by its use of trellis-work and rustic furnishings, both of which are easily and cheaply made at home. Furniture for summer breakfasts and afternoon teas should be simple wickerwork or rattan.

To capture the spirit of the cottage garden, it is essential to plant borders in the traditional 'patchwork' method employed by our predecessors: plants were swopped or grown from seeds and scattered at random to grow where they would. This planting produces a charming informal effect and, by turning to the old-fashioned varieties now offered again by seed merchants, the simplicity of the cottage garden of yester-year can easily be recaptured.

IN AN ENGLISH COUNTRY GARDEN
Time to relax – after hanging out the day's washing, a task made more pleasant by using our pretty patchwork and appliqué peg bag

PEG BAG

ALWAYS USEFUL, the peg bag has suffered from being poorly produced and designed. This peg bag, however, would look attractive hanging on any clothes line and would make a welcome gift for a friend.

MATERIALS

small piece of card
scissors
ruler
HB pencil
0.5m/½yd of 90cm/36in white cotton fabric
1m/1yd of 90cm/36in contrasting cotton fabric
sharps needle
toning sewing cotton
white embroidery thread
small piece of tracing paper
1 wooden coathanger
hacksaw
2B pencil

MEASUREMENTS

Finished size is 32.5 × 30cm/12¾ × 11¾in

METHOD

1 Make a patchwork template by cutting out an 8cm/3in square from the card.
2 Iron the white cotton fabric flat and, using the template, draw 28 squares on the wrong side of the fabric.
3 Cut each of these squares in half diagonally, making 56 pieces in all.
4 Repeat steps 2 and 3 using the contrasting cotton.
5 Make each patchwork square by joining one triangle of white cotton with one of contrasting cotton (diagram 1). Sew by hand or machine and press seam open (55 squares).
6 Piece together 5 squares in rows, making 11 strips altogether. Machine seams and press open.
7 Stitch all the strips together to form a rectangle measuring approx 38 × 84cm/15 × 33in. Press open seams.
8 Place the finished patchwork over the contrasting cotton and using this as a pattern, cut a lining piece of fabric.
9 With right sides together stitch around three sides leaving open one 38cm/15in side. Trim corners and turn right side out.
10 Turn in hem allowance on raw edges and slip stitch neatly together.

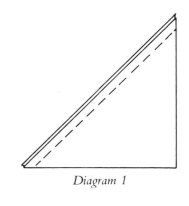

Diagram 1

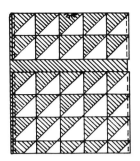

Diagram 2

11 Fold the rectangle: bring the bottom edge upwards so that 3½ patchwork squares are showing and bring the top edge downwards showing 2 patchwork squares (diagram 2), thus forming 2 pockets. Stitch seams neatly.

12 Make a small hole in the top middle of the 2 square pocket and blanket stitch using white embroidery thread to stop fraying. Slide coathanger

Blanket stitch

into this pocket, allowing the hook to come through the hole. If the coathanger is a little too big, saw a fraction off each end.

13 To transfer the word 'Pegs' to the contrasting fabric, trace from the diagram using a 2B pencil and tracing paper. Turn over and redraw the letters on the other side of the tracing paper. Turn over again and place on the fabric. Draw over the word 'Pegs' again, thus transferring the design to the fabric. Cut out around letters carefully.

14 Cut a piece of white fabric 15 × 9cm/6 × 3½in to make a panel and turn in and tack a narrow hem all round.

15 Tack 'Pegs' on to the middle of this panel and blanket stitch using white embroidery thread all around letters.

16 Stitch panel centrally on the bottom pocket.

PAINTED HOUSE SIGN

THERE ARE MANY house signs on the market today and it is an easy matter to choose one in a style that will complement your house and reflect your personality. However, with a little time and effort, it is possible to create your own 'masterpiece', which will express your individuality to the world and add character to your home.

In the true spirit of the thrifty Victorian cottage-dweller, recycling where possible, we have utilised a redundant kitchen-unit door and, having been given a new lease of life, it proudly announces the name of our ideal country cottage home.

MATERIALS

1 panelled wood kitchen-unit door
medium and fine sandpaper
white undercoat
very light green matt emulsion paint
paintbrushes
pencils
stiff card (optional)
scissors
tracing paper
acrylic paint in various colours, including white (for goose)
ruler
paints
clear varnish
mounting hooks and screws

MEASUREMENTS

Finished sign measures 60 × 45cm/24 × 18in

METHOD

1 Using first the medium and then the fine sandpaper, rub down the door until it is smooth and clean. Wipe over with a damp cloth. Leave to dry and then

121

wipe over thoroughly with a dry cloth.

2 Now paint the entire surface with a thin coat of light green emulsion. Leave to dry thoroughly and repeat until an even covering has been achieved.

3 Next, transfer the goose design above. Draw a pencil grid on to the door panel, making the squares as large as necessary to fit your particular panel. Using these squares as a guide, draw the goose. Alternatively, draw your own design straight on to the card. Keep the design simple for maximum impact. Remember, the sign is designed to be seen from a distance and fine detail will therefore be lost. Cut around the goose shape or your own design, and, using this as a template, draw the pattern (including edgings) on to the door as shown.

4 Trace the letters required for your house name on to tracing paper (see alphabet on pages 124–5). Decide where you will place them and mark the centre of the door. Then, starting from the middle of the name, place letters in position and draw over again, thus transferring the letter shapes to the door. Paint the design first and then the letters, adding some decorative flowers if desired. Leave to dry completely.

When the design is finished, seal with two thin coats of varnish. Attach mounting hooks with screws provided and hang in position.

FIRST IMPRESSIONS
*A hand-painted house sign gives a very
personal welcome to visitors*

A B C D

J K L M

R S T U

Z 2 3 4

124

EFGHI
NOPQ
VWXY
56789

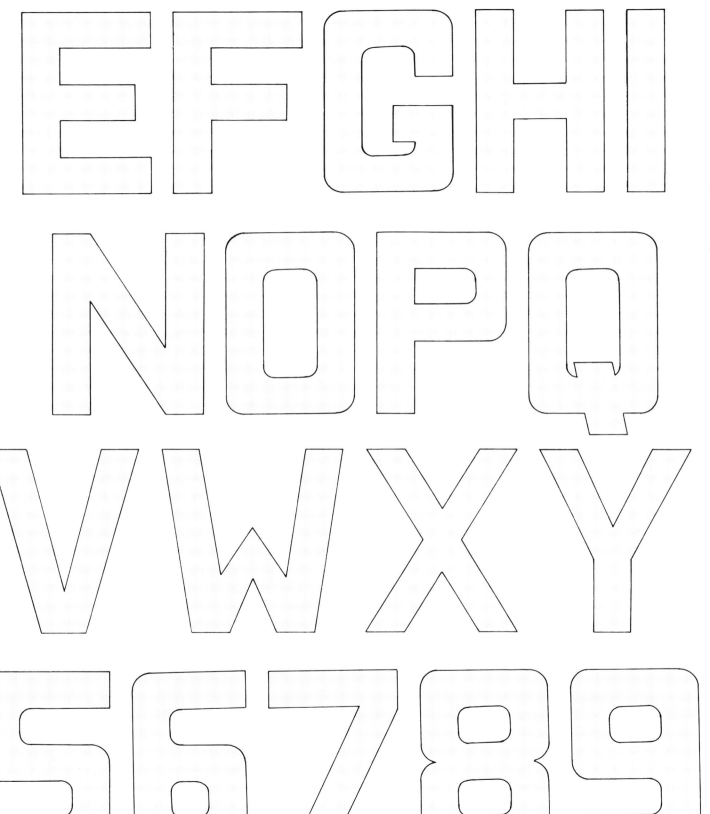

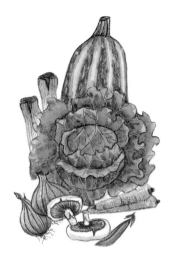

SUNDIAL

Sunshine and love don't last
Enjoy them while you may

A SMALL AMOUNT OF woodwork is required to produce this timepiece, but the finished result is well worth the effort involved.

MATERIALS

medium sandpaper
rectangular piece of wood, measuring 1.5 × 1m/3 × 2ft
pale green/grey undercoat paint
pale green/grey emulsion paint
15cm/3in paintbrush
ruler
alphabet stencil
lead pencil
small pot each of dark green, blue and dark red paint
selection of small fine paintbrushes
optional tracing paper
selection of suitable acrylic paints
wood batten 7.5 × 5 × 22.5cm/3 × 2 × 9in
wood batten 5 × 2.5 × 22.5cm/2 × 1 × 9in
PVA wood glue
clear matt varnish

MEASUREMENTS

Finished measurements are 1.5 × 1m/3 × 2ft

METHOD

1 Sandpaper the wood lightly to smooth the surface and apply a coat of green undercoat. Leave to dry. Apply a further coat of green or grey emulsion and leave to dry again.
2 Using dark green paint and household paintbrush, flick paint at the board to produce a mottled effect.
3 Draw two light pencil lines 7.5cm/3in and 15cm/6in down from top edge of wooden rectangle and, using the alphabet stencil, draw out the motto at the top of the page along these lines.

4 Using the red paint and a small paintbrush carefully paint in the letters. Paint the outline of each letter first before filling in. Leave to dry thoroughly.
5 Down each long edge of the board, draw a selection of leaves and stems. These can be drawn very simply as this will add charm to the finished sundial. This border should measure approx 10cm/4in and be placed 7.5cm/3in in from outer edges.
6 If you feel it is impossible to draw a freehand design, try tracing a suitable pattern and transfer this to your borders. Paint, using a selection of natural paint colours. Leave to dry thoroughly.
7 It is now necessary to paint in the hour lines of the sundial. Measure approx 29cm/11½in down from top edge of board and mark the centre point. Through this centre point draw a parallel line 20cm/8in long. Draw a further parallel line 5cm/2in lower and a third line 25cm/10in lower. Draw a perpendicular line from each end of this line upwards to meet the top line, thus forming a rectangle measuring 20cm × 30cm/8in × 12in.
8 From the centre point of the second line from the top draw an arc with a radius of 5cm/2in, as can be seen in the photograph.
9 Mark the centre point of the arc and the lower line of the rectangle and draw a perpendicular line to connect the two.
10 Now, using a protractor to mark angles of approx ten degrees along the arc, mark off five radiating lines on each side of the perpendicular line (eleven lines in all). Extend these lines to the edge of the rectangle and pencil in.
11 These lines should then be painted in very carefully, using a fine brush and the dark blue paint.
12 Using the alphabet stencil, mark in the hours in Roman numerals. Paint as before and leave to dry thoroughly.
13 When paint is completely dry, varnish with clear matt varnish. Leave to dry and revarnish at least once.

SUNSHINE & LOVE
DON'T LAST

ENJOY THEM
WHILE YOU MAY

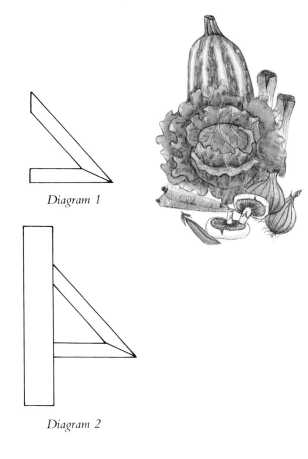

Diagram 1

Diagram 2

*This attractive ivy-clad wooden sundial
with its traditional verse is
surprisingly easy to make*

14 Measure in 45cm/18in from each edge of the board and mark this point 30cm/12in down from the top edge. The battens should be glued together at an angle (diagram 1) and glued to the board at this point (diagram 2). Leave to dry for 24 hours.

15 The sundial is now ready to hang in position on a south-facing wall by whatever means you choose to employ.

127

GARDENER'S APRON

MATERIALS

sheet of graph paper measuring 91.5 × 66cm/36 × 26in
pencil
scissors
pins
1m/1yd of 90cm/36in wide green fabric, either a heavyweight
cotton or linen
reel of matching green sewing cotton
sharps needle
tape measure
140cm/1½yd of 4cm/1½in wide green or black tape
tracing paper
stencil card
stencil brush
small jar of dark red or contrasting fabric paint
craft knife

MEASUREMENTS

This apron will fit up to a 34in waist

METHOD

1 Using the grid pattern shown in the diagram on page 130, draw the apron shape on to the graph paper; 1 square is equal to 5cm/2in.

2 Cut out this paper pattern and pin to right side of fabric. Using this as a guide, cut out the apron shape.

3 Out of the remaining fabric cut two rectangles: 1 × 56 × 20.5cm/22 × 8in and 1 × 25.5 × 20.5cm/10 × 8in, for the pockets.

4 Turn over and hem along both long edges on each pocket, leaving both side edges raw.

5 Pin the two pockets into position, turning in raw edges on smaller pocket; the large pocket should be placed 20.5cm/8in up from the bottom edge of the apron; the smaller one 15cm/6in down from the top edge. Tack into position. Machine sew smaller pocket.

6 Turn in a 1.5cm/½in hem all round the apron (including the edges of the larger pocket) and machine stitch hem.

7 Place the apron on a flat surface and, using a pencil, measure and mark pocket divisions, as shown in the diagram.

8 Machine these divisions as shown, or decide where you wish your own divisions to be placed and machine stitch accordingly.

9 Measure the length of the neck strap required and cut out a piece of tape, allowing an extra 5cm/2in for overlap. Machine stitch into position at each top corner of the apron (see diagram).

10 Divide the remaining piece of tape in half and use to form waist ties. Machine stitch firmly into position at each outer corner.

11 Press apron thoroughly, before proceeding to step 12.

12 Using the alphabet shown in the 'Painted House Sign' project on pages 124–5, make a stencil as described on page 104.

13 Using fabric paint, stencil the words 'GREEN FINGERS' on to the apron. Alternatively, the stencil could be used as a guide to draw on the letters with a pencil. These could then be painted in using a small brush and a variety of fabric paints.

14 Set the fabric paint as recommended by the manufacturer (normally by using a warm iron over the letters).

This apron could be further personalised by adding the wearer's name or the house name across the top pockets.

GREEN FINGERS
With lots and lots of pockets, our hardwearing gardener's apron is utterly practical

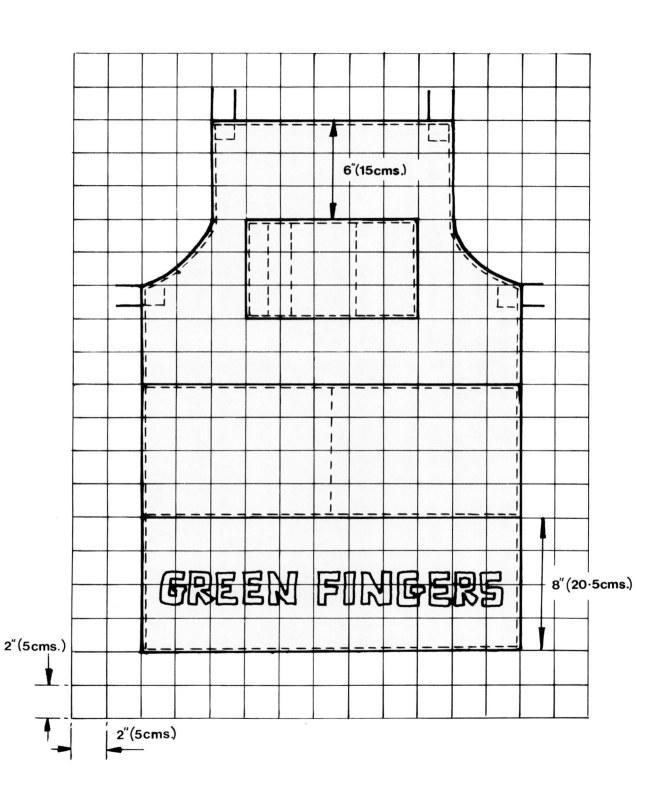

6″(15cms.)

GREEN FINGERS

8″(20·5cms.)

2″(5cms.)

2″(5cms.)

FLOWER POT NAME MARKERS

Wᴵᴛʜ ᴛʜᴇɪʀ ᴘᴀꜱꜱɪᴏɴ for decorating absolutely everything, the Victorians would purchase little, brightly painted ceramic name markers for their pot plants. Here the modelling medium Fimo has been used to produce a set of markers, which would look especially cheerful in herb pots on the kitchen windowsill.

Fimo modelling medium in assorted colours
rolling pin
sharp knife
baking sheet
sheet of foil
small piece of tracing paper
pencil
Fimo varnish

MEASUREMENTS

Finished measurement is approx 13.25 × 4.5cm/5¼ × 1¾in

METHOD

1 Make a template by tracing the marker shape on to paper. Cut out.
2 Roll out Fimo in your chosen colour to approx 0.3cm/⅛in thickness.
3 Place the paper template over the Fimo and cut around using a sharp knife. Smooth the edges.
4 Using a contrasting colour, make a long sausage (approx 0.3cm/⅛in diameter) by rolling the Fimo backwards and forwards with your fingers on a flat surface.
5 Place this strip all around the edge of the pattern shape, leaving the spiked end free.
6 Make another thinner sausage and carefully place on to the marker to form the plant name.
7 Lay the marker carefully on to the baking sheet, which has been covered with foil. Bake for 20–30 mins at 130°C. Leave until completely cold.
8 Varnish with Fimo varnish, using at least two coats.

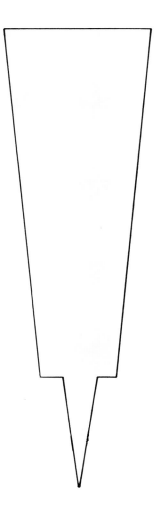

131

HAMMOCK

W HEN ALL THE WORK is done in the garden, what could be more pleasant than relaxing in a hammock slung between two ancient trees? (Be careful, however, that the branches chosen will support the weight!) This hammock is made of macramé and is easy and quick to complete.

MATERIALS

150m/150yd 8mm coarse string or cord
a broom stave cut in half
4 drawer knobs in light wood

METHOD

1 Out of the coarse string cut 9 lengths, measuring 15m/49ft; 2 lengths measuring 1m/39in; 2 lengths measuring 175cm/5ft 9in; 2 lengths measuring 470cm/15ft 3in.

2 Find the centre point of each of the 9 long cords and using the 2 × 175cm/5ft 9in cords work a line of flat knots (see diagram) over all 9 cords for 40cm/16in. Begin either side of centre point and work outwards to the left and right.

3 Using one of the 1m/39in lengths work a wrapping knot* (see diagram) over all cords for 7½cm/3in.

Wrapping knot

* Wrapping knot: form a loop with one end of the cord. Wrap the cord around the centre cords (including the loop) and place end through loop. Pull down on loop base, pulling loop inside. Cut ends.

4 Spread out the cords and starting 28cm/11in from the wrapping knot, double half-hitch (see diagram) the centre cord to one length of broom stave. Con-

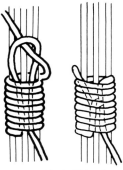

Double half hitch

tinue to attach the other cords in the same way, increasing the distance from the wrapping knot to the stave until the last cord attached at either side is approx 36cm/14in away. The broom stave should be perfectly level with the cords forming a fan shape above it (see diagram).

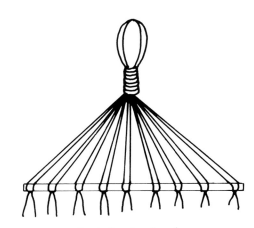

Cords forming fan shape

5 Take one of the 470cm/15ft 3in cords and fold it in half. Mount it with a lark's head to the far left of the stave (see diagram) immediately next to the first double half-hitch. Mount the second cord in the same way to the right side of the stave. These cords are known as bearing cords and will remain straight whilst working.

Lark's head

6 Leaving aside the bearing cords, the remaining cords will be numbered 1–18 from left to right.

7 Slant cord 1 to the left and, leaving 5cm/2in of unknotted cord, work 1 double half-hitch over the bearing cords.

8 Slant cord 2 to the right and repeat step 7 with cord 3.

9 Repeat step 7 along row, working right hand cord over the left.

10 Slant cord 18 to the right and leave 5cm/2in of unknotted cord work 1 double half-hitch over the right bearing cords.

11 Slant cord 18 to the left and leaving 5cm/2in of unknotted cord work 1 double half-hitch over it with cord 17. Repeat this step all along the row, this time working the left-hand cord over the right.

12 Repeat steps 7–11 until work measures 2m/2¼yd from the broom stave.

13 Leave 5cm/2in of unknotted cord and double half-hitch each cord to the second piece of broom stave with double half-hitches. Tie each pair of bearing cords together with 2 overhand knots, cut close and, using PVA wood glue glue firmly in place.

14 Fan the remaining cords to match the beginning and using the remaining 1m/39in of cord tie an 8cm/3in wrapping knot over all cords (see diagram).

15 Divide the cords into 2 groups of 9 cords and work each group as follows: Take 2 cords and work a line of flat knots for 32cm/12½in over the remaining

Flat knots

7 cords. Hold all 9 cords together and tie 1 large overhand knot. Cut the cords to 48cm/19in from the overhand knot and tie an overhand knot at the end of each cord (see diagram).

Overhand knot

16 Screw a drawer knob into the end of each piece of broom stave and the hammock is ready to hang in position, tied firmly at both ends.

PATCHWORK CUSHIONS FOR A HAMMOCK OR GARDEN CHAIRS

PATCHWORK WAS ORIGINALLY devised to utilise scraps of fabric, pieced together to make a whole. As log cabin patchwork uses quite a lot of fabric, it can also be worked in a variety of ribbons. The effect of these cushions is further enhanced by using the same fabrics in a variety of patchwork styles.

LOG CABIN CUSHION

MATERIALS

medium-weight card
pencils
ruler
set square
craft knife
brown paper
remnants of dark, small-print cotton fabrics
remnants of light, small-print cotton fabrics
43cm/17in square of calico
43cm/17in square of heavyweight wadding
0.5m/½yd printed cotton fabric for cushion back
tacking cotton
sharps needle
waxed quilting thread
2m/2yds piping cord (optional)

MEASUREMENTS

Finished size is 41 × 41cm/16 × 16in

METHOD

1 Make a 2.5cm/1in square template. Now make 8 more templates, adding 5cm/2in to the length each time. The final template should measure 43 × 2.5cm/ 17 × 1in. For each template (except the first 2.5cm/ 1in square – cut 3) cut out 4 paper rectangles. Use these templates to cut out shapes from brown paper to line cotton patchwork pieces.

2 Using the printed cotton remnants, cut 1 dark and 2 light 2.5cm/1in squares. Then cut 2 dark and 2 light rectangles from each of the rectangular templates, except for the template measuring 42.5cm/17in × 2.5cm/1in. From this template cut 2 dark rectangles only.

3 Using brown paper pieces as templates, turn in a small hem on each cotton patch and tack down, making sure corners are right-angles.

4 Lay out all the pieces as shown in the diagram, building up the pattern as you work.

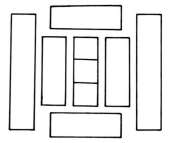

AFTERNOON NAP
A selection of colourful patchwork cushions, including the log cabin design, invite the gardener to take it easy in this traditional hammock

5 Stitch patches together by machine or by hand, working from the centre square. If working by hand, put two patches right sides together and oversew neatly along one edge. Try not to sew through the paper. If machine sewing, place two patches side by side and zigzag together.

6 Finish with the last two dark rectangles. The patchwork square will measure 42.5cm/17in approx.

7 Place the square of calico on a flat surface and cover with wadding. Lay the patchwork square on top right side uppermost and pin through all layers securely around all edges. Tack firmly into position.

8 Using waxed thread hand quilt along all seams. Alternatively, using a matching thread, machine stitch along all seams.

9 From backing fabric cut two rectangles measuring 42 × 25.5cm/17 × 10in. Turn in a 1.25cm/½in hem along one long side of each rectangle and machine stitch.

10 Overlap the two rectangles to produce a rectangle measuring 42.5cm/17in, the two hemmed edges forming a pocket. Pin in place.

11 Place right sides of patchwork and backing fabric together and tack together. Machine stitch a 2.5cm/1in seam all round.

12 Cut across corners and turn right side out.

13 Slip stitch piping cord in position around seam line, if required.

14 Press lightly and insert a cushion pad.

Using the above basic instructions for assembling the cushion, make a selection of cushions using the following patchwork techniques. These can be quilted in the same manner as the log cabin patchwork or left plain, in which case no wadding or muslin will be required.

GRANDMA'S FLOWER GARDEN

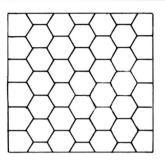

TUMBLING BLOCKS

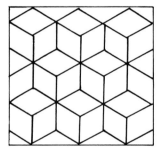

The tumbling blocks design has been popular in Britain since the eighteenth century. To be successful this pattern must be made up from a selection of light, medium and dark shades. The lightest shade should be used on the top surface of the block, the darkest on the right side and the medium on the left. This sequence should be used throughout the design to give the impression of light falling on the three-dimensional blocks.

ENGLISH KNITTED COVERLET

ENGLISH KNITTED QUILTS have been famous for two hundred years and those that have survived show a great ingenuity of pattern, although the basic motifs are always fairly simple to work. The pattern given here is called Apricot Leaf and this has been teamed with a traditional Feather Pattern border. For your coverlet, choose a pastel colour that will complement the patchwork cushions, for a completely coordinated look. The sample pictured below has been worked in an ecru shade, which shows its textured patterning to advantage.

The pattern is built up of large squares, each composed of four smaller squares, which are knitted from corner to corner and then sewn together. The size of the coverlet will depend on the number of squares you choose to work.

A QUIET MOMENT
A traditional knitted coverlet will keep out summer breezes as you relax with a good book in our scented cottage garden

MATERIALS

12 × 100g balls of Twilleys Lyscordet cotton in ecru set no 10 knitting needles

MEASUREMENTS

Finished measurement is 91.5 × 91.5cm/36 × 36in

ABBREVIATIONS

st – stitch
sts – stitches
k – knit
p – purl
m1 – make a stitch
psso – pass slip stitch over
dec – decrease
tog – together
sl 1 – slip stitch
rep – repeat

137

METHOD

To work the motifs

Begin by casting on 2 sts.

1st row: K1, m1, k1.

2nd row and each alternate row unless otherwise stated: P.

3rd row: (K1, m1) twice, k1.

5th row: (K1, m1) 4 times, k1.

7th row: K1, m1, p1, k2, m1, k1, m1, k2, p1, m1, k1.

8th row: P2, k1, p7, k1, p2.

9th row: K1, m1, p2, k3, m1, k1, m1, k3, p2, m1, k1.

10th row: P2, k2, p9, k2, p2.

11th row: K1, m1, p3, k4, m1, k1, m1, k4, p3, m1, k1.

12th row: P2, k3, p11, k3, p2.

13th row: K1, m1, p4, k5, m1, k1, m1, k5, p4, m1, k1.

14th row: P2, k4, p13, k4, p2.

15th row: K1, m1, p5, k6, m1, k1, m1, k6, p5, m1, k1.

16th row: P2, k5, p15, k5, p2.

17th row: K1, m1, p6, sl 1, k1, psso, k11, k2 tog, p6, m1, k1.

18th row: P2, k6, p13, k6, p2.

19th row: K1, m1, p to centre panel, sl 1, k1, psso, k to last st, m1, k1.

20th row: P, k and m sts and k p sts of previous row. Rep last 2 rows 4 times.

29th row: K1, m1, p12, m1, sl 1, k2 tog, psso, p12, m1, k1.

30th row: P.

31st row: K to end, inc 1 st each end of row (31 sts).

32nd and 33rd rows: As 30th row.

34th row: K2 tog * m1, k2 tog, rep from * to last 3 sts, m1, k3 tog.

35th row: P.

36th row: P, dec 1 st at each end of row.

37th row: K.

38th row: As 36th row.

39th row: P.

Rep rows 34–39 inclusive 3 times and then rows 34–37 inclusive once more (3 sts remain).

P3 tog and fasten off.

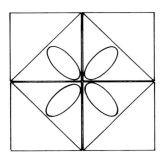

Diagram 1

Make sufficient squares to produce a coverlet of the desired size and sew up as shown in diagram 1.

To work the border

The border is knitted separately and then sewn to the coverlet. Extra length must be allowed for 'easing' around corners (approx 10cm/4in for each corner).

Cast on 35sts.

1st row: P.

2nd row: K.

3rd and 4th rows: As 1st and 2nd rows.

5th row: K1, * m1, k6, k2 tog, sl 1, k1, psso, k6, m1, k1 rep from * to end.

6th row: P.

7th to 16th rows: Rep 5th and 6th rows 5 times.

These 16 rows form pattern. Repeat as required. Cast off and sew around coverlet. Finish off by working a single knotted fringe.

To work the fringe

Cut lengths of yarn 30cm/12in long, fold in half and using a crochet hook knot them in bunches of eight through the border edge at 5cm/2in intervals. Make the decorative fringe by knotting once at 5cm/2in intervals (diagram 2).

Diagram 2

A BUTTERFLY GARDEN

ONE OF THE JOYS of living in the country is the opportunity it gives for encouraging wild creatures into the garden to share its delights. Of course, this does mean that the cabbages are sampled by the caterpillars of various butterflies, but this seems a small price to pay for the pleasure that delicate butterflies bring on a warm summer day.

We all nostalgically remember the summer days of our childhood: the wild flowers, butterflies, hedgehogs and shrews, and the soporific hum of bees. It is possible for us all to do something positive to preserve the wildlife of our lovely countryside, by providing a little oasis of food and shelter. The smallest garden can, for very little financial outlay or physical effort, be turned into a mini nature reserve and the gardener can be assured that any efforts will be amply repaid.

Food must be offered to passing butterflies, in the form of nectar-bearing flowers, and once eggs have been laid caterpillar food must also be available.

Plants for caterpillar food are:

ash	dandelion	plum
beech	dock	poplar
birch	elm	privet
blackthorn	fennel	scabious
bramble	gorse	sorrel
buckthorn	hawthorn	spurge
burdock	hop	thistle
cabbage	horseradish	willow
carrot	lime	willowherb
cherry	nettle	
clover	oak	

Some of the plants particularly loved by butterflies are:

ageratum	dandelion	michaelmas daisy
alyssum (white)	everlasting pea	petunia
arabis	foxglove	phlox
aubrieta	globe thistle	polyanthus
bluebell	golden rod	primrose
buddleia	heather	sea holly
(butterfly bush)	hebe	sedum
campion	heliotrope	sweet rocket
candytuft	honeysuckle	sweet william
cineraria	lavender	thrift
clover	lilac	thyme
comfrey	mallow	valerian
cowslip	marigold	verbena
daisy	marjoram	wallflower

A FINAL THOUGHT...

OUR IDEAL COUNTRY COTTAGE is now complete and it is time to relax and admire the results of our hard work. How pleasant it is to accept the compliments of friends, marvelling at the skill required to produce such a welcoming and original home! For on a warm summer day, what could be more delightful than relaxing in a handmade hammock, under the shade of the apple and damson trees, a traditional Victorian coverlet to keep out chill breezes over the knees and a beautiful patchwork cushion at your head?

Perhaps it is time to plan another project!

ACKNOWLEDGEMENTS

Grateful thanks to Beatrice Smith for working the rag rug on page 19. To Judi Lang for the needlepoint firescreen on page 47. To Jean Batterbee for the florentine work footstool on page 52. To Joy Rowe for the sleep cushion on page 107. To Lesley Doram for the instructions for making the silk-covered box. Heather Smith for working the crochet curtain on page 15. Lesley Coleman for working the knitted lace for the tablecloth on page 85. Cathy Elson for providing the lovely patchwork cushions featured on page 135. Dave Wiggall for his woodworking advice and the men at Timboard in Burton on Trent for their patience while cutting and sawing wood to our instructions! To our agent Dianne Coles for all her help and for putting us in touch with Jon Davison and Philip Millington Hawes, who have provided such wonderful photographs. To Sarah Widdicombe and Brenda Morrison at David & Charles for all their help and advice in the production of this book. To Hilary Allison, Barbara Hair and Joan McKinnon for the loan of precious items for photographing and to Alan Greenman and Simon Lings for the authors' photographs on the jacket.

May we offer our thanks to Mrs Allison for allowing us to photograph the immaculate and beautiful cottage garden of her home, which is featured here in the hope that it will serve as a small tribute to her late husband's gardening skills.

Also to Pamela Harper and her staff at Twilleys of Stamford Ltd, especially Brenda Francis and Queenie Frisby. Some of the projects featured in this book are available in kit form from Twilleys of Stamford Ltd, Roman Mill, Stamford, Lincs PE9 1BG (Tel (0780) 52661, Fax (0780) 652215, Telex 32518 Twilly G). For further information send a stamped addressed envelope. In the USA these kits can be obtained from Scotts Woolen Mill, PO Box 1204, 528 Jefferson Avenue, Bristol, PA 19007.

And finally, to all our friends who have encouraged us with their interest and support over the past years – thank you from both of us.

ABOUT THE PHOTOGRAPHER

Jon Davison is an Oxford-based photographer and publisher, who moved to the UK from his native New Zealand in 1980. Jon's work is primarily the interpretation of mood and atmosphere and it is this, plus his graphic sense of colour, that makes him an internationally respected lensman.

As well as the images he has produced for this book, his other specialist areas are travel and aviation and these form the basis of his publishing activities. He is married with two children and enjoys skydiving as a leisure activity.

INDEX

Learne to leave one worke, and to learne another,
For here they may make choice of which is which,
And skip from worke to worke, from stitch to stitch,
Until in time, delightfull practice shall
(With profit) make them perfect in them all.

Thus hoping that these workes may have this guide,
To serve for ornament, and not for pride.
To cherish vertue, banish idlenesse,
For these ends, may this booke have good successe.

John Taylor
'The Prayse of the Needle'